KNOCK IT OFF!

HOW TO QUIT BEING A JERK @ WORK

DR. GUYLA J. GREENLY

979-8-9851154-0-6 D2D
979-8-9851154-4-4 IngramSpark
979-8-9851154-1-3 KDP ebook
979-8-9851154-2-0 KDP print

Edited by Self Publishing Services
selfpublishingservices@gmail.com

Cover Design by Renata Strauss
Interior Layout by Renata Strauss

Dedication

*For my kids: Geoff Cooper, Jeanna Cooper Smith,
and Michael Thayer. You know I have a song lyric
for everything, and you can imagine my choice.*

Acknowledgment

It is impossible to put a project like this together single-handedly. So many people encouraged me, prayed for me, held me accountable to deadlines, allowed me to tap into their expertise, and shared their "you won't believe this" stories. I would like to thank each of them, but that just might add up to enough pages to equal another book. Instead, if you're reading this and you helped out even in a small way, please know it was huge to me.

Now, for some specific acknowledgments. I so appreciate:

My Doctoral Project Prayer Team: Suzi Cooper, Gayle Irwin, and KPaul Maurer. There were days when I didn't think I could research or write another word. You answered my SOS texts immediately with much-needed encouragement. Thank you for keeping me lifted before the Lord.

My illustrator: Rachel DeMaere Reilly. You did an incredible job of taking what I saw in my head and putting it in perfect pixelation. I'm so glad you get my sense of humor. I LOVE what you came up with, but not as much as I love YOU.

My project chair: Dr. Diane Wiater. I can't even. I do not have adequate words to express how much knowing you has improved me. In the words of the Apostle Paul, "I thank my God upon every remembrance of you."

My fellow professional women: Alyssa Thayer, Amy White, Kate Rice, Kyleen Braxton, Kaitlin McGuire, Liz Waldron Knight, Neva Bodin, and Gayle Irwin. Thanks for sharing your funny stories, frustrations, and wealth of wisdom. And thanks for listening to me talk out these ideas, helping me work through edits, and for your overall cheerleading. You each inspire me.

My editor: Clare Wood. Thank you for walking me through this publishing process and keeping the whole project moving forward despite my propensity for self-sabotage. We embarked on this project during difficult seasons for each of us. Thanks for listening, encouraging, and keeping me laughing.

as someone who has been on all sides of the hiring process, has trained job seekers, and worked with employers in hiring those seekers, I say, "way to go Dr. Greenly!"

Diane M. Wiater, Ph.D.
Strategist, coach, leadership development,
and small-business consultant
Wiater Consulting Group, LLC

———

Knock it Off! is a delightfully humorous yet hard-hitting, to-the-point, get-yourself-together life manual for anyone ready to come to terms with replacing limited thinking and self-sabotage with action-oriented unlimited potential. Reflective of her own Values in Action (VIA) Inventory of Character Strengths and Virtues attributes, Guyla's book mirrors her VIA character strengths of humor, honesty, love, spirituality, and love of learning. Guyla makes you laugh at yourself as she speaks truth into wrong thinking and offers common-sense solutions by uncomplicating the obvious. She presents a number of assessment and coaching tools to familiarize the reader with their strengths and attributes and guides them toward new realities in self-appreciation, self-care, and self-love. This is a comprehensive guide written with the purpose of helping readers land the career and job of their dreams, yet it could easily be a book on how to live life to the fullest. She leaves no rocks unturned with helpful reminders and tips all the way down to tuning into body language. Guyla's book will make you laugh, cry, and think carefully about the meaningful aspects of life as well as those concealed leverage points we may be inclined to ignore. This book has wide application as a self-help kick-starter with sound entrepreneurial business and marketing strategies fused with just enough humor and tough love to motivate readers to take the necessary steps to land a new job, become indispensable, and exit well when it is time to move on to the next adventure.

Virginia Richardson, DSL
Business and healthcare futurist, graduate professor,
and board-certified business coach
Foresight Center

———

During some point in our lives, most of us have worked with a jerk at work ... or been one ourselves. In her new book, *Knock it Off! How to Quit Being a Jerk @ Work*, Dr. Guyla J. Greenly helps those new to the workforce, those seeking a new career, and those in leadership roles understand the importance of being professional ... no matter the profession. From attitude and appearance to appreciation language understanding, and appropriate behaviors, her insights not only help you get and keep a job but also propel you toward a sustainable career to where your supervisor will regret your departure when you decide to leave. Using sensible tips and research studies, true stories and logic, all interlaced with humor, Dr. Greenly expands horizons for employees, potential employees, and employers. With a "Checklist for Success" woven amid the pages, she offers opportunities for readers to evaluate themselves —no matter where they work or want to work. I highly recommend this astute, educational, and practical book!

Gayle M. Irwin
Author/Author-Mentor/Freelance Writer
Casper, Wyoming
www.gaylemirwin.com

TABLE OF CONTENTS

ARE YOU A JERK @WORK?

Generally, when we hear the word jerk, we think of someone who is rude, crude, annoying, bullying, arrogant, dismissive, or argumentative. The list of adjectives is seemingly infinite and always negative, and often describes deliberate behaviors. You may not identify as a jerk, and maybe you're not.

Buuuuut …

Do you think it's possible for others to think you're a jerk for reasons you never even thought about or for behaviors you didn't realize were upsetting to others? Maybe you are a jerk at work and you don't even know it! Perhaps you don't have a job right now, so you're thinking, "I can't be a jerk at work because I don't go to work!" Think about this: maybe you're being a jerk in your job search, and that's keeping you from getting hired.

The first step in learning how to quit being a jerk at work is to assess your level of jerkiness. (Is that even a word? Let's say it is.) Once you realize you have a jerkiness problem, you can take steps to knock it off! Read through the *Are You a Jerk @ Work Checklist* below and put a checkmark next to each item that describes you.

Are You a Jerk @ Work Checklist

☐ I don't have a résumé.

☐ I do have a résumé, but it's outdated and incomplete, and may have a typo or two. (OK, maybe more, I haven't proofread it.)

☐ If a job listing requires a cover letter, I either send a résumé and refuse to include a cover letter, or I don't bother to apply at all.

☐ If I do send a cover letter with my résumé, I keep it simple so I can use the same documents for every job I apply for.

☐ I have no idea what my strengths are.

☐ I rarely, if ever, check my email or voice messages.

☐ I don't answer my phone. Just text me.

☐ I answer my phone all the time, even if I'm in the middle of a job interview. You never know, it could be an emergency.

☐ I take a lot of selfies at work.

☐ I complain about my current or previous job, boss, and coworkers on social media.

☐ I make a lot of "I can't wait for the weekend!!" and "OMG, it's Monday already" posts on social media.

☐ I'm always running late, but it's OK because I make it up over lunch or at the end of the day.

☐ I live by the statement, "My life, my rules."

- ☐ I believe if you want my respect, you have to earn it.

- ☐ I'm not afraid to tell you exactly what I think.

- ☐ Everybody gets into arguments at work. It's no big deal.

- ☐ I'm a super casual person and it doesn't matter what I wear to work; I'm still a hard worker.

- ☐ I love chatting with my coworkers and take every opportunity to keep up with all the company gossip.

- ☐ Sometimes I bring stuff home from work, like notepads or extra toilet paper. They'll never miss it.

- ☐ I like to bring leftovers for lunch, heat them up in the microwave, and eat at my desk. My favorite lunch items include fish, raw onions, lots of garlic, strong cheeses, brussels sprouts, and hard-boiled eggs.

- ☐ I enjoy playing pranks on my coworkers, especially when they repeatedly tell me to stop.

- ☐ I have a lot of piles, sticky notes, dirty dishes, empty takeout containers, crumbs, and other stuff in my work area.

- ☐ I am an open book and tell my coworkers what's going on in my personal life. After all, everyone needs an opportunity to vent, and we spend a lot of time at work!

- ☐ My friends and family need me and often call me at work or drop by to say hi.

☐ Sometimes I don't feel like going to work, so I take a personal health day and ask a coworker to cover for me.

☐ If there's a task my boss wants me to do that I don't like, I just won't do it.

☐ I never refill the water in the coffee maker if I'm the last to use it. I also leave my pod in the machine and a dirty spoon on the counter along with spilled sugar and creamer.

☐ I use the last of the toilet paper or paper towels and don't replace the empty roll.

☐ I watch videos at full volume on my phone at my desk.

☐ I discuss politics and religion at work even though I don't work in politics or at a faith-based organization.

SCORING

0-5: You're a saint. No one is perfect, but you're pretty close. You likely get along well with your boss and coworkers and are a valued employee. Depending on your company culture, some of the items on the list may not have applied to you.

6-10: You're mildly annoying. A few too many typos, being overly chatty, or being a bit arrogant may irritate a coworker or two, but overall you're a good worker.

11-20: You're obnoxious. More than mildly annoying, you are downright obnoxious. Whether unwittingly or deliberately, you are doing your best to drive those around you insane! You probably feel ignored by your coworkers or wonder why they often seem short with you. You test their patience. You likely haven't received a merit-based raise or promotion in a while, and your supervisor has given you at least one warning about your behavior and performance.

21-30: You're a jerk—at least at work. You're rude. You have a bad attitude and a lousy work ethic. You struggle to find and keep a job but, as evidenced by the fact you picked up this book and took the quiz, you don't want to remain a jerk. You're ready to knock it off and stop being a jerk at work.

INTRODUCTION

My first job was ironing dress whites for my dad and the other sailors in our neighborhood. I was ten years old, and I was bringing in the big bucks! Twenty-five cents for each item. Pressing military uniforms is tedious work. It's essential to make the creases in precisely the right places and smooth out every last wrinkle. The sailors—and their wives—were more than happy to outsource the chore at such a bargain rate.

As I got older, I moved on to classic employment opportunities, such as babysitting neighborhood kids and flipping burgers down at the fast-food joint. If you've ever worked at McDonald's or somewhere similar, you have a pretty good idea of what my job entailed. It was the classic teenage entry-level position: part-time work for minimum wage. It was at that locally owned diner where I set myself apart from my workplace peers. While the other employees stood around talking and laughing between customers, I washed walls, scraped gum from under the tables, and disinfected the soda machine taps. The owner noticed and transferred me to his downtown restaurant, where I worked full-time and earned tips. I spent the next year waiting tables and covering the grill, earning enough money in tips alone to pay cash for my first car—$500 for a used Chevy Citation.

Have you figured out yet that, by some standards, I am OLD? I fall into the elusive unicorn generation called Gen X. Those of us born between 1965 and 1980 are a small (about 65.2 million) group of people squeezed in between the two enormous and oft-heralded baby boomer and millennial generations. We are the original "latchkey kids," the independent ones who came home after school to an empty house. If our parents were still together, they both worked. Some of our parents raised us alone. We babysat our younger siblings, did our homework without prompting, started dinner, and set the table. We hung out in malls, saw the first video on MTV ("Video Killed the Radio Star" by The Buggles), and watched every John Hughes movie. We can tell you where we were and what we were doing when John Hinckley Jr. shot President Ronald Reagan, and how we felt when President Reagan said, "Mr. Gorbachev, tear down this wall!"

According to a 2018 article in *Fast Company* magazine, Gen X leaders hold 51 percent of leadership roles globally. We are the people for whom you are working. Because we spent so much time in our developmental years exercising our freedom to make decisions and organize our time while our parents worked, we grew into adults with entrepreneurial and independent management styles. We expect our coworkers and direct reports to do the same.

As members of the "sandwich generation," we take care of our aging parents while launching our kids into the world and becoming grandparents. We have a lot on our plates, and the last thing we want to do in the workplace is to take care of you. We expect you to be independent adults who don't need micromanaging. We don't mind mentoring; in fact, we kind of dig it, but we already raised our kids. We don't want to raise you, too. By writing this book, I hope to teach you the basics so you can go into a job ready to manage yourself well, which will benefit you, your manager, and your company as a whole.

In the thirty-plus years since my first job, I have worked in corporate and nonprofit management, and I've gathered a bit of education from universities as well as the school of hard knocks. I went from elementary school-age clothes-presser to CEO of a statewide trade organization, and I am now a doctor of strategic leadership (DSL) with my own coaching and leadership development business. I won't bore you with my résumé, but let's just say I know a thing or two because I've seen a thing or two (cue Farmers Insurance Group commercial music).

I have put my experience and education, along with the wisdom of friends and colleagues with decades of experience in hiring and managing employees, into the pages of this book. You can read it in order all the way through, or you can read just the chapters covering the issues you find essential at this time. You'll find cartoon illustrations scattered throughout and a checklist at the end of each chapter so you can assess how you're doing in the subject covered. I have also scattered **Soapbox Alert** sections throughout the book. When you see this image, you'll know you're in for a rant on an issue that drives employers crazy.

You may read some things in this book that offend you, annoy you, or strike you as just plain stupid. You may be tempted to toss the book aside and pronounce it rubbish. If that happens, will you accept this challenge? Take some time to think about why you had an emotional reaction to what you read. It's OK if you disagree with me; I'll still appreciate you for giving my thoughts a chance. But please don't just dismiss the tips in here without first giving them some serious consideration.

A few years ago, I had offers for two job opportunities within one week, even though I wasn't looking for employment. A friend who was job searching said, "I just don't get it. I'm putting applications in all over town and can't find a job, but you get two job offers in one week just sitting at home." I didn't want to hurt his feelings, but there are particular reasons why I get jobs and excel in the workplace, and he does not. I don't want to hurt your feelings either, but if you are struggling to the point of picking up this book and at least flipping through it, know that I can help you up your game in the world of work. Why not give it a shot?

SECTION ONE:
YOU GOTTA KNOW YOURSELF TO SELL YOURSELF

You've taken the Are You a Jerk @ Work quiz and gained a bit of insight into your level of jerkiness. But you might not understand why some of the items you checked are annoying or how to improve your work performance. If you stick with me, you'll find the answers ahead on this journey from jerk to saint. The first step is self-awareness. A study commissioned by Green Peak Partners Organizational Consulting and conducted by a research team at Cornell University identified the top criterion for success. The report stated, "A high self-awareness score was the strongest predictor of overall success."

Having self-awareness means you have knowledge of yourself. You understand your habits, likes, dislikes, the way you view the world, and your needs. You know what you want in life and have an understanding of your emotional responses. Having self-awareness doesn't solve your challenges in life, but it gives you an accurate starting point and allows you to develop a game plan for solutions. Without self-awareness, you're doomed to repeat your mistakes for the rest of your life, staying stuck in the jerk-at-work rut.

Before you can sell yourself to a potential employer, you need to know what qualities, strengths, and skills you have to offer. Do you know the answers to the following questions?

- What are you good at?

- What do you love doing?

- What do you hate doing?

- What are your strengths and weaknesses?

- What energizes you, and what stresses you out?

The better you understand yourself and how you're wired, the better you will perform and thereby excel in the workplace. In the next three chapters, I will show you how you can discover and understand your personality type, language of appreciation, and top strengths.

1. What's Your Type?

The first time I ever heard of personality type was when the pastor who led our premarital counseling asked my fiancé and me to take the Myers-Briggs Type Indicator personality inventory (MBTI). The pastor said it would help us better understand ourselves and our compatibility. My result was ESFJ; his was INTP. ESFJ stands for extravert/sensor/feeler/judger, and INTP stands for introvert/intuitive/thinker/perceiver. Basically, I'm someone who lives life out loud. I gather information from my five senses, make decisions based on how they affect others, and have a healthy respect for time and deadlines. He, on the other hand, lives mostly inside his head, stores his interpretation of data rather than the details, makes decisions based on pros and cons, and takes a more casual approach to time and deadlines. I guess it's true; opposites really do attract.

I have since taken the MBTI three more times as part of various leadership or employee development initiatives. I have also taken the 16Personalities.com free personality test and the TypeCoach Verifier. The result is always ESFJ. I've even tried changing some of my answers to see if I get a different result. Nope. Still an ESFJ.

This piqued my curiosity, so I set out to learn about personality theory. I still have a lot to learn, but I am now a master certified facilitator of TypeCoach, a tool for understanding personality types.

So, what do letters like ESFJ and INTP mean and how does that knowledge help you get a job and do well in the workplace? Read on to find out.

First, Some History

Personality is a combination of behaviors, emotions, motivation, and ways of thinking by which each individual is defined. The study of personality is called personality psychology, and it evidently began waaaaayy back in the days before Jesus with Hippocrates's theory of the four humors. It's kind of gross, but ancient Greek philosophers thought our personality and temperament were determined by the strengths of certain bodily fluids called humors. The four humors are blood, black bile, yellow bile, and phlegm. If you've ever heard of the four temperaments sanguine, melancholic, choleric, and phlegmatic, then you've heard of this ancient theory. It remained popular through medieval times and even influenced the work of Russian psychologist and physiologist Ivan Pavlov. (Remember Pavlov's dogs and their reactions to the sound of a bell? Yeah, that guy.) Many other psychologists and philosophers have also studied the concept of personality, including Sigmund Freud (the id, ego, and superego dude from psych class), Abraham Maslow (hierarchy of needs), and Carl Jung.

Jung introduced the theory of psychological types in the 1920s. Isabel Briggs Myers and her mother, Katharine Briggs, expanded on Jung's research and began to create the MBTI in 1942. They took Jung's concepts and developed a four-letter method to conveniently describe the order of each person's Jungian preferences. After two decades of research and testing, Myers and Briggs published the type indicator (MBTI) in 1962. To date, millions of people around the world have taken it.

The ease of using the four-letter naming model developed by Myers and Briggs led to its use by varying theories and approaches. One approach is 16 Personalities. In their description of their framework (www.16personalities.com/articles/our-theory), they listed Socionics, David Keirsey's Temperament Sorter, and Linda Berens's Interaction Styles as examples of diverse approaches. They further explained that although the four-letter acronyms in each system "may be identical or very similar," their meanings are not always the same.

It is my recommendation, therefore, that you choose a theory to learn, and then stick with it, so you don't receive conflicting or confusing information.

I am a big fan of TypeCoach, which you might already have guessed because I mentioned I have a master's certificate in it. The platform and teachings are closely related to Carl Jung's theories and Myers and Briggs's teachings. Rob and Carly Toomey developed TypeCoach. On their website, www.type-coach.com, they stated they have "spent more than 50,000 hours studying the topic and application of personality type in organizations." Their type verifier and subsequent trainings build on personality type theory to "deliver practical applications of personality type to drive business results." The rest of the information presented in this chapter, unless noted otherwise, was developed from my training in TypeCoach.

Second, What Do the Letters Mean?

Each letter has a counterpart, creating four two-letter sets. Each two-letter set represents a specific part of the human personality. Both Myers-Briggs and TypeCoach refer to these as preferences. All people use all preferences, and all preferences are equal. The Myers-Briggs's website states that all types are equal; there are no "good" or "bad" types, and no type is better than another.

TypeCoach holds the same belief and teaches that type is similar to handedness. We have two hands, and we use both hands, but most of us have a preferred hand we use the most. This is called our dominant hand. It is the hand we use most naturally, but it does not stop us from using our other hand. In fact, we can train ourselves to become adept at using both hands.

I developed a severe case of carpal tunnel syndrome when I was in high school. The doctor put me in a splint and told me not to use my right arm for six weeks. I wasn't to brush my hair or teeth, write, type, or even carry my books with my right arm. It was a challenge, but I developed a decent ability to write with my left hand and type with only my left hand. I've since reverted to being dominantly right-handed, but I still use my left hand more often and more adeptly than I did before having carpal tunnel syndrome.

I was always able to use my left hand; I just got better at using it in tasks for which I hadn't previously used it. It's the same with the eight preferences. We have and use all of them, but there are some we naturally use more often. We are, however, able to train ourselves to get better at using the others and to employ them more frequently.

TypeCoach also teaches the concept that ALL types can do ALL jobs, though some aspects of every job just come more naturally to various personality types. By becoming aware of our personality types and our natural tendencies, we can better understand why we excel at some things and struggle with others. Armed with this knowledge, we can train ourselves to both hone our natural strengths and improve our lesser tendencies.

THE 8 PREFERENCES

The Eight Preferences

The eight preferences are paired into four categories that indicate how individuals gain energy, process information, make decisions, and respond to structure. Although many people think of the preferences as either/or extremes, each person actually falls somewhere on a sliding preference scale. TypeCoach created *The 8 Preferences* graphic, and it is a great tool for visualizing preferences and better understanding the scale concept. To illustrate the scale, consider my daughter (ESFP), daughter-in-law (ENTP), and me (ESFJ). We are all extraverts, but we each feel most comfortable in different areas of the scale between extravert and introvert. My daughter is further to the left (see photo), I'm further to the right (closer to an introvert), and my daughter-in-law falls somewhere in the middle. By the same token, my two sons and my son-in-law are all introverts who fall on different points of the scale. One son (ISTJ) is sometimes mistaken for an extravert. He is further to the left on the scale. I used to think my other son (ISTP) was to the far right as an introvert, until I met my son-in-law (ISTJ). They are both closer to the right on the scale, but one is almost as far right as possible.

Now that you know we all have and use all preferences and that we fall somewhere on a sliding scale, let's take a deeper look at each pair.

E/I, Extravert or Introvert: Energy

One of my biggest pet peeves is that people seem to think extravert means outgoing and introvert means shy. Trust me when I say there are plenty of shy extraverts and outgoing introverts in the world. Rather than describing how comfortable you are in a crowd, E/I is all about energy—how you recharge and what tends to drain you. In their book, *Type Talk: The 16 Personality Types That Determine How We Live, Love, and Work,* Otto Kroeger and Janet M. Thuesen wrote that E/I deals with "the way people prefer to interact with the world and the way they prefer to receive stimulation and energy."

The population is divided evenly between extraverts and introverts. Remember, everyone switches back and forth between introvert mode and extravert mode, but depending on their natural tendencies, they will default to their preferred mode.

Here are some traits of each type:

EXTRAVERT	INTROVERT
Gains energy from the outside world	Recharges by spending time in their inner world
Talks more than listens	Listens more than talks
Talks to work out what they think	Thinks, then talks, then thinks some more
Is quick to respond	Pauses to think before responding
Is likely to interrupt or finish sentences	Will not work their way into a conversation, and if interrupted too many times, will simply stop talking

S/N, Sensor or Intuitive: Information

The S stands for sensor, and N stands for intuitive. We already used I for introvert, so it couldn't be used again without a great deal of confusion. Therefore, we use the word's second letter, N. The sensor and intuitive functions are related to how we take in and process information. Kroeger and Thuesen called them the "two ways people prefer to gather data." According to TypeCoach, about 65 percent of the population are sensors and 35 percent are intuitives. Sensors gather information through their five senses and store the raw data in their mental file cabinets or hard drives. When they need the information, they can pull out the raw data, analyze it, and come to a conclusion. Intuitives, on the other hand, focus on big-picture ideas and future possibilities. They take in the raw data, extract their conclusions, and file away their impressions.

Check out this list of common S/N traits:

SENSOR	INTUITIVE
Is energized by executing concrete and clear tasks	Is energized by brainstorming ideas and vision setting
Asks specific how questions	Seeks the big picture
Notices and remembers details	Remembers the gist of things
Has great memory for detail, especially for conversations	Shuts down when others verbally vomit too many details
Speech patterns include using short sentences, lots of specifics, and clear language. Asks for clarity.	Speaks in longer, sometimes run-on, sentences; shares their thinking rather than details; speaks in general and uses original analogies

T/F, Thinker or Feeler: Decisions

Everyone thinks, and everyone feels. The two are not mutually exclusive. Just like with the other preferences, we flow back and forth between the thinker and feeler modes but default to our dominant preference. Thinkers and feelers are also divided equally among the population. People automatically assume that men are thinkers and women are feelers. In many cases, they might be right! This is the only dimension with a gender bias: 60 percent of men lean toward thinker, and 60 percent of women lean toward feeler.

Check out this list of common T/F traits:

THINKER	FEELER
Naturally weighs pros and cons	Naturally weighs impact on others
Makes decisions based on objective logic	Makes decisions based on their values
Makes decisions with their head	Makes decisions with their heart
Naturally direct and assertive	Naturally diplomatic and empathetic
Critiques to solve problems first	Praises to show support first
Is naturally "thick-skinned"	Is likely to be more easily hurt or offended

J/P, Judger or Perceiver: Structure

Our final category often confuses people when they hear the terms for the first time. When people hear the word *judger*, many automatically say, "Oh that's me; I'm always judging people." Others are offended when they get their verifier results and see the word, thinking to themselves, "But I'm not judgmental!" Others say, "Oh, I'm a P because I'm very perceptive." Judger and perceiver actually have to do with our preference for structure and how we think about plans and time. Approximately 60 percent of people are judgers, while 40 percent are perceivers.

Check out this list of common J/P traits:

JUDGER	PERCEIVER
Is structured	Is spontaneous
Seeks closure	Likes to leave options open
Is time-conscious, makes plans	Is casual with both time and plans
Works first, plays later	Mixes work and play
Feels urgency and stress with deadlines	Enjoys the rush of winging it at the last minute

The Sixteen Types

These eight preferences combine into sixteen personality types. There are eight extravert types and eight introvert types. Technically, it would also be correct to say there are eight sensor types and eight intuitive types, or thinker and feeler types, or judger and perceiver types. But because E or I is the first letter in all personality types, we break them into these two categories for easy reference. When you take the MBTI or TypeCoach Verifier, you receive a lengthy report about your specific type. Many books also go into detail about each type. Because this is just one chapter in a book on a wider subject, I included adjectives used by TypeCoach to describe each type and the one-sentence description for each type from *Type Talk* by Kroeger and Thuesen.

ESTJ—Life's administrators. Logic-driven, straightforward, dependable, decisive, tenacious, proactive, high-energy, take-charge, fast

ESFJ—Hosts and hostesses of the world. Enthusiastic, sympathetic, warm, sensitive, generous, attentive, responsible, talkative, affectionate, outgoing

ESTP—The ultimate realist. Talkative, inventive, observant, active, charming, practical, get-it-done, take-charge, hands-on

ESFP—You only go around once in life. Sensitive, easygoing, fun, talkative, kinesthetic, entertaining, sympathetic, free-spirited, in the moment, casual

ENTJ—Life's natural leaders. Bold, assertive, strategic, tenacious, take-charge, decisive, innovative, confident, high-energy, proactive with a tendency to learn more

ISTJ—Doing what should be done. Methodical, responsible, loyal, literal, precise, clear, meticulous, reserved, accurate, realistic

ISFJ—A high sense of duty. Reserved, precise, decisive, private, literal, sensitive, sympathetic, planful, efficient, accommodating

ISTP—Ready to try anything once. Logic-driven, private, quiet, spontaneous, level-headed, concise, in the moment, unflappable, down-to-earth, realistic

ISFP—Sees much but shares little. Quiet, unassuming, observant, sensitive, kind, private, free-spirited, spontaneous, reserved, in the moment

INTJ—Everything has room for improvement. Intense, independent, future-focused, private, tenacious, intellectual, deep, reserved, direct, driven

ENTP—One exciting challenge after another. Creative, adaptable, strategic, independent, unconventional, clever, skeptical, funny, tenacious

INTP—A love of problem-solving. Private, original, internally motivated, witty, analytical, logic-driven, unconventional, disorganized, independent, skeptical

ENFJ—Smooth-talking persuader. Creative, empathetic, planful, affectionate, sensitive, idealistic, talkative, visionary, values-driven, charismatic

INFJ—An inspiration to others. Planful, private, sensitive, reserved, visionary, empathetic, idealistic, value-driven, conscientious, perfectionistic

ENFP—Giving life an extra squeeze. Spontaneous, sensitive, visionary, imaginative, idealistic, energetic, insightful, collaborative, gregarious

INFP—Performing noble service to aid society. Calm, reserved, caring, casual, modest, sensitive, spontaneous, empathetic, unique, flexible

In his article "Psychological Types in Freud and Jung," John Beebe advocated understanding the theory of psychological types so one is better able to "appreciate individual differences and to recognize the different types as valid starting places for adaptation." He warned that to be "unaware of the types is to risk unnecessarily pathologizing what may actually be adaptive and healthy."

The topic of personality type can appear overwhelming. I'll admit, it's a lot to take in and a lot to cover at an introductory level in a single chapter. To help simplify things, let me share a short list of things I particularly want you to take away from this chapter:

- There are no right or wrong or good or bad personality types. All are equal. All are valuable.

- No two people are exactly alike, and the sixteen personality types should never be used to put people in a box. They are a guideline to help us better understand ourselves and improve our communication with others. The descriptions of each personality type are generally true, but they will vary from person to person because of many factors, including these:

  - Life experiences

  - Level of preference (remember the discussion about sliding scales)

  - Personal choices: One ESFJ might choose, for example, to work on developing thinker preferences while another ESFJ chooses to develop intuitive preference.

- Personality type assessments should NEVER be used to discriminate against others. Tools such as the MBTI and TypeCoach Verifier should not be used to prescreen or eliminate applicants or discourage anyone from pursuing any type of career.

When you learn to identify your own type and read the type clues of those around you, you can tailor your approach to quickly engage with and expand your influence with others. Think ahead to when you're sitting in a job interview. How might you use this information to your advantage? Here's one possible scenario. If you know that you are an extravert and that you have a tendency to interrupt and try to complete others' sentences, be aware of it. Practice listening more and talking less. Listen to your interviewer, allow her to finish her sentence, and then give an answer.

Don't interrupt. Practice mastering this skill in your everyday life. It will improve your relationships with bosses, coworkers, family, and friends.

Perhaps you're intuitive. Now that you understand this preference a bit more, you can be aware of your tendency to use long, run-on sentences and speak in general terms. Prior to a job interview, practice answering questions with shorter sentences, giving specifics instead of generalities. Or perhaps you're a sensor. Sensors tend to be uncomfortable with open-ended questions, and most interview questions are open-ended. So, if you're a sensor, try practicing answers to common interview questions such as "Tell me about yourself" or "Why do you want to work for this company?"

Communication is vital to any relationship, be it personal or professional. Understanding personality types can help you get your message across so others hear it and help you hear and understand their messages. One of my fellow TypeCoach professionals, Pam Rechel of Brave Heart Consulting, summarized the importance of communication in the workplace when she stated, "If you can't communicate, stuff can't get done."

If you want to quit being a jerk and get hired or excel in the workplace, learning to communicate is vital for your success. Understanding personality types in general, and your type specifically, will increase your ability to effectively communicate. To learn more about personality types try one or all of the following:

- Read books on the subject

- Visit www.type-coach.com to learn more

- Visit www.myersbriggs.org to learn more

- Work with a coach (like me www.dandelionleadershipcoaching.com) to take an assessment and learn how to interpret and apply the results

How Am I Doing? Checklist for Success

☐ I have taken an assessment, such as the TypeCoach Verifier or MBTI.

☐ My four-letter personality type is _______________

____

☐ I am best able to recharge my energies when I _______________

____

☐ My greatest challenges with how I process information (intuitive or sensor) in the workplace have been _______________

____

☐ Now that I understand my personality type and how I process information, I can better handle my related challenges by _______

____

____

☐ Do I have a balanced approach to making decisions, or do I lean too far in either direction (intellect over emotion, or emotion over intellect)? _______________

☐ How can I practice using my dominant decision-making personality factor (thinker or feeler) in a beneficial way in the workplace? _____

____

____

☐ How has my relationship to time and deadlines (judger or perceiver) impacted my work output and relationships with my boss and coworkers? _______________________________

____

____

☐ Now that I better understand my relationship to structure, I can improve my performance at work and my relationships with bosses and coworkers by _______________________________

____

____

2. What Are Your Strengths?

In my humble opinion, people spend too much time focused on their weaknesses, wallowing in self-pity over how those perceived weaknesses hold them back from living the life they think they want. I've been known to wallow in that pit of despair myself. When I went through a divorce, I bought into the lie that all single mothers are impoverished, overworked, and unfulfilled. I'm not sure where I heard that fallacy. I assume from society, but I suspect it came from my deepest fears.

When my kids were in upper elementary and junior high school, and I was working a full-time job, volunteering in church, and working on a master's degree, I hired a house cleaner. I felt so guilty. I told my sister I didn't deserve to spend my money that way. I was a single mom. Life should be harder. She tried not to laugh at me and instead told me I could not delegate parenting, I couldn't delegate earning a living, and I couldn't delegate advancing my education, but I could outsource cleaning my house. As usual, she was right. I got over myself and enjoyed the extra time that delegation of work allowed me.

I have since slayed other monsters of limiting beliefs like these:

- I'm too fat to have fun at the beach. (Apparently only model-thin people are allowed to have fun. And guess what. My granddaughter is not giving my appearance a single thought. All she knows is that Gramma Guyla helps her build awesome sandcastles and find the best seashells.)

- I'm bad at math, so I won't be successful with bookkeeping and budgeting in my new job. (Ummm, I'm great at adding and

subtracting and thinking in categories. Bookkeeping doesn't require calculus).

- I need to be perfect before I can help others be better. (Duh, no one is perfect—not even me, no matter how much I want to be. If I were perfect, you probably wouldn't want to hear what I have to say anyway).

- I hate conflict, so I can't be a good manager of employees. (I still hate conflict, but I've learned how to have difficult conversations in ways that are authentic to my personality and strengths).

Did you catch that last statement? I *learned* how to become better at something by honing my *strengths*. You see, when we focus on our weaknesses, we become weaker. When we concentrate on our strengths, we become stronger. If I thought only about how much I hated conflict, I would have become conflict-avoidant, instead of conflict-averse. I still dislike conflict. But instead of avoiding it, I have accepted that it is a fact of life and that it is my duty as a leader to face conflict swiftly so it doesn't get out of control. Rather than focusing on conflict aversion as a weakness, I chose to accept my abilities to be diplomatic and empathetic as strengths and use them when facing uncomfortable conversations.

I want you to take this message to heart. Read it again. Meditate on it. Absorb it. Stop dwelling on all the things you think you're not good at or can't do. By dwelling, you're giving power to your weaknesses and limiting beliefs. Train your mind to turn from the negative and stare boldly into the face of your strengths. If you're a human with an iron will, channel it! Make it your greatest strength. The Hulk under control is a powerhouse hero, but out of control, he is destructive and toxic.

As you read the rest of this chapter, start thinking about your character strengths and skills. Make note of your strengths and hang onto the list. You'll need these later when you start writing your résumé and preparing for interviews.

Tom Rath is a consultant on employee engagement, strengths, and well-being. He is best known for his extensive research and studies on strengths-based leadership. Several of his books were required reading in my doctoral program. The first sentence of the first chapter of *Strengths-Based Leadership* by Rath states, "If you spend your life trying to be good at everything, you will never be great at anything." He further states,

"Without an awareness of your strengths, it's almost impossible for you to lead effectively."

"Wait a minute!" you might be thinking. "I'm not a leader. I'm just trying to get a job."

Yes. You are a leader. Take a look at all the things you manage: relationships, hobbies, volunteer work, tasks, yourself. Whether you lead yourself well or poorly is up to you. But I'm guessing you're looking to be a great self-leader because you're reading this book. If you didn't want to lead yourself into a better work life, you would never have picked it up.

Somewhere in your bucket of strengths is the capacity to be a good leader, and you'll likely find it by concentrating on your positives instead of the negatives. That approach is the cornerstone of positive psychology. In their 2014 article in *Marketing Education Review,* University of Wisconsin professors Chuck Tomkovick and Scott R. Swanson wrote, "Positive psychology focuses on the building of human strengths, positive behavior, and virtues rather than the deficits in human nature such as weaknesses, victimology, and psychological problems."

Positive Psychology

Clinical psychologists, psychiatrists, and social workers use classification schemes to classify and diagnose patients. Their focus is on weaknesses and pathologies. NOTE: I'm not saying traditional psychology is bad and positive psychology is good. This is not an either/or conversation. Rather, I am attempting to help you understand the differences between the two schools of thought. There are circumstances where one form of psychology is more appropriate than the other. If I'm exhibiting psychotic tendencies, I need a traditional psychologist to help me figure out my symptoms and diagnose and treat me. But if I need to create a personal brand and market myself to advance my career, discovering my unique strengths is fundamental to that goal.

Let's take a look at why it's a good idea for all of us to focus on our strengths.

- It builds self-confidence. Rath said, "It is hard for us to build self-confidence when we are focused on our weaknesses instead of our strengths." A coaching client came to me feeling defeated, questioning whether she had what it takes to successfully manage a team. She struggled to deal with a whole staff of jerks! Her daughter, a part-time employee in her business, was with us during the first session. I asked the client if she let her daughter get away with being disrespectful to her and doing whatever she wanted to when she was a teenager. They both laughed, snorted, and in unison said, "NO!" I simply said, "So you do have a backbone?" She laughed and agreed. After several months of working together, she is remembering that she does have valuable strengths that empower her to run a successful business.

- There is lifetime value in knowing your strengths as early in life as possible. According to Rath, "People who are aware of their strengths and build self-confidence at a young age may reap a cumulative advantage that continues to grow over a lifetime." Understanding and capitalizing on your strengths as early as possible in your life will have an impact on the whole of your life similar to the impact of compound interest: saving and investing earlier leads to a bigger nest egg when you retire.

- Individuals can derive purpose in their lives by establishing awareness of their singular strengths.

- Understanding one's strengths can foster a greater sense of identity and self-confidence. When the CEO position opened at the company where I was the executive assistant, I questioned whether I should apply. I kept focusing on the strengths of the previous CEO and comparing myself to her. I called a previous employer and asked if she thought I was qualified. She told me I'd had the ability from the beginning. I didn't see my own strengths or trust myself until someone else told me I was better than I thought I was. Through this experience I learned to focus on MY strengths, not someone else's. I applied and got the job and thrived for seven years in the position before deciding to pursue new challenges.

- Employees who use their strengths at work handle their workloads more effectively and show a lower level of absenteeism.

- Employees who are encouraged to use their strengths in the workplace experience higher levels of vitality, flow, passion, and engagement.

- Research indicates employees who identify, use, and develop their strengths at work tend to perform better and are more proactive in the workplace. Jerks at work are not as self-aware as their saint counterparts. Have you noticed coworkers, or even yourself, constantly making negative comments? These people are focused on weaknesses instead of strengths.

Are you convinced yet? I hope so because we're moving on to talk about two assessments you can take to help you identify your strengths. The first is a paid assessment focused on identifying talents and skills in the workplace. The second assessment is free and helps us understand what's best about us as human beings. Both focus on positive qualities in the individual and help shift attention from weaknesses and deficits toward the strongest and best qualities in people. Taking both assessments allows you to develop a more well-rounded picture of your strengths and increases your overall level of self-awareness.

CliftonStrengths Talent Assessment

No, that is not a typo: there is no space in the official title of the CliftonStrengths Talent Assessment. Educational psychologist Donald Clifton invented the Clifton StrengthsFinder (another one that doesn't use a space). According to Rath, "The strengths philosophy is the assertion that individuals are able to gain far more when they expend effort to build on their greatest talents than when they spend a comparable amount of effort to remediate their weaknesses." Clifton received an American Psychological Association Presidential Commendation naming him the "father of strengths-based psychology." Since his death in 2003, Clifton's StrengthsFinder has undergone a name change. For the remainder of this section, I'll refer to it as the assessment.

Rath defined the assessment as "an online measure of personal talent that identifies areas where an individual's greatest potential for building strengths exists." According to research reported by Gallup (the company that now owns the assessment), researchers identified thirty-four strengths that "naturally cluster into four domains of leadership strength."

EXECUTING (Making things happen)	INFLUENCING (Reaching broader audiences)	RELATIONSHIP BUILDING (Fostering working together)	STRATEGIC THINKING (Thinking about what could be)
Achiever	Activator	Adaptability	Analytical
Arranger	Command	Connectedness	Context
Belief	Communication	Developer	Futuristic
Consistency	Competition	Empathy	Ideation
Deliberative	Maximizer	Harmony	Input
Discipline	Self-Assurance	Includer	Intellection
Focus	Significance	Individualization	Learner
Responsibility	Winning Others Over (WOO)	Positivity	Strategic
Restorative		Relator	

When you take the assessment (there is a fee, but this is your career after all), you will receive a report that identifies your signature themes, your top five strengths. The report will include a paragraph explaining each theme.

My signature themes are communication, responsibility, WOO, individualization, and input. When I received this report, I thought, "What?! I'm not a woo girl!" I didn't know what WOO meant. My immediate impression was that it referred to people who go around whooping and hollering and getting people riled up, like a cheerleader. I am far more reserved than that.

I soon found out that WOO actually stands for *winning others over*, and it means I am good at meeting new people and finding an immediate connection. The report stated, "You actually enjoy initiating with strangers because you derive satisfaction from breaking the ice and making a connection." OK, when you put it that way, I get it and embrace it as part of my strengths. I can now see how WOO has helped me build relationships quickly and easily. After Laurie Lye interviewed me for a position at Casper College Library, she told me I interviewed well because I appeared comfortable and personable. I have since been told by others that I interview well. I attribute that to my strengths of WOO and communication. I encourage you to take a few minutes at the end of this chapter to list your top five strengths and brainstorm how each one will help you either get or keep a job. How will focusing on these strengths help you move up the ladder from jerk to saint?

Many books, articles, and other related information are readily available to take you deeper into the strengths philosophy, but you'll get the best explanations from taking the assessment. You'll find everything you need to discover your CliftonStrengths at www.gallup.com/cliftonstrengths.

VIA Classification of Character Strengths and Virtues

The Values in Action (VIA) Inventory of Character Strengths and Virtues is a newer assessment that's been made available for free by VIA Institute on Character. According to the VIA website (www.viacharacter. org), "The study of strengths started in the early 2000s when scientists gathered to study character more scientifically. A total of 55 distinguished scientists joined the study over several years."

Their studies resulted in the VIA assessment that measures twenty-four character strengths. The strengths are grouped into six classes of virtues:

WISDOM	COURAGE	HUMANITY	JUSTICE	TEMPERANCE	TRANSCENDENCE
Creativity	Bravery	Love	Teamwork	Forgiveness	Appreciation of Beauty and Excellence
Curiosity	Perseverance	Kindness	Fairness	Humility	Gratitude
Judgment	Honesty	Social Intelligence	Leadership	Prudence	Hope
Love of Learning	Zest			Self-Regulation	Humor
Perspective					Spirituality

VIA defines character strengths as "capacities humans have for thinking, feeling, and behaving in ways that benefit oneself and others." The authors assert that everyone has all twenty-four strengths, but some people express some strengths more naturally than others. A person's top five character strengths are referred to as signature strengths—just like CliftonStrengths. What determines whether a strength is signature is whether the strength is "essential or core to who the person is." These are the strengths that matter the most to you. They are the most central to your personal identity; when someone thinks of one of these strengths, they think of you.

My top five VIA character strengths are humor, honesty, love, spirituality, and love of learning. I had never thought of humor as a strength. But VIA materials classify humor as a transcendence virtue and define it as "liking to laugh and tease; bringing smiles to other people; seeing the light side; making (not necessarily telling) jokes." Most humor occurs in the moment and happens organically. Humor can help make difficult tasks more tolerable or simply make work more fun. Back when I worked at Casper College Library, we had an imaginary employee named Bambi. When someone made a silly mistake or when something unexplained happened, we blamed it on poor Bambi. August and September were always stressful times at the association as we prepared for the annual state conference. One day one of my coworkers came across a meme that showed a little girl making a funny face. The caption read, "I frickin' love spiders." I frickin' love (insert whatever) became our new catchphrase. We laughed about our frustrations, saying things like, "I frickin' love last-minute cancellations!"

What if I consider the VIA character strength of humor in relationships along with the CliftonStrengths' theme of WOO? As I stated earlier, winning others over is the ability to break the ice with strangers and quickly find common ground. Neurohumorist Dr. Karyn Buxman said,

"Humor enhances communication, bonds teams, improves retention, increases productivity, and improves profitability." My top CliftonStrength is communication. The use of humor enhances communication and bonds teams. Now that I am aware of my strengths of humor, WOO, and communication, it is easier for me to understand how they work together to help me make connections with people at work and foster a positive work environment.

When we combine the knowledge gained from both tools, we can gain a full picture of our natural patterns of thinking, behaving, and feeling; our core virtues and values; and our top talents and skills. I encourage you to keep an inventory of your personality type, CliftonStrengths, and VIA Character Strengths. Use the checklists at the end of each chapter to capture this valuable information and develop your self-awareness. You'll need this information to become a more well-rounded human and a successful employee.

If you marked "I have no idea what my strengths are" on the Jerk @ Work Checklist, I hope you've taken this chapter to heart. If you take time to take each assessment and fill in the information in the following checklist, you can erase that checkmark and move one step further from jerk and closer to saint.

How Am I Doing? Checklist for Success

☐ I have taken the CliftonStrengths Talent Assessment
(https://www.gallup.com/cliftonstrengths/en/home.aspx).

☐ My top 5 strengths are these:

1) ____

2) ____

3) ____

4) ____

5) ____

☐ How have I used each of these strengths in previous work, school, or volunteer capacities?

____

____

____

____

____

____

☐ How can I use each of these strengths in my current position?

____

____

____

____

____

____

☐ How can I highlight these strengths on my résumé?

____

____

____

____

____

☐ How can I highlight these character strengths in an interview?

____

____

____

____

____

☐ I have taken the VIA Character Strengths assessment (www.viacharacter.org).

☐ My top five VIA Character Strengths are these:

1) _______________________________________

2) _______________________________________

3) _______________________________________

4) _______________________________________

5) _______________________________________

☐ How have I used each of these character strengths in previous work, school, or volunteer capacities? _______________

____

____

____

____

____

☐ How can I use each of these character strengths in my current position?

____

____

____

____

____

____

☐ How can I highlight these character strengths on my résumé?

____

____

____

____

____

____

☐ How can I highlight these character strengths in an interview?

____

____

____

____

____

____

☐ Now that I know my top strengths, I am prepared to answer the popular interview question: "Tell us about your strengths." I have written out a response to this question: _______________________

____

____

____

____

____

3. Appreciation Languages

What happens when your car's fuel tank is nearly empty? As long as your fuel gauge is working properly and you remember to look at it, you will receive warnings so you can work in a trip to the gas station. If your gauge is broken or you ignore the warning light, your vehicle stops operating.

But that's not all that can happen. When my sister's friend Sam borrowed her car, he stopped at the gas station to refill the tank before he returned it. Having grown up with a similar vehicle that ran on diesel, he assumed Jerri's car took the same fuel. He filled the gas tank, but it didn't get him very far. Seems a gas engine won't run on diesel. A well-intentioned show of appreciation turned into a disaster.

The same can happen with people. In the preface to the 2012 edition of *The 5 Languages of Appreciation in the Workplace,* Dr. Gary Chapman wrote about how he discovered over an eighteen-year period of marriage and family counseling that everyone has a "love tank" that must be regularly refilled. Loved ones might try to show their love to a person, but if they don't use the right "fuel" to fill the "tank," the recipient runs out of gas. For example, one of my friends used to get irritated that her husband frequently told her that he loved her, that she was beautiful, and so on. I was astounded that she would complain about that and asked why it bothered her. She said that she was sick of hearing it and that words don't mean anything. The couple eventually divorced because her love tank was not filled with the right fuel. She didn't need the words; she needed the actions. Not receiving them, she ran out of gas.

Chapman realized that what makes one person feel loved doesn't necessarily make another person feel loved. He also realized people best receive love in five significant ways: words of affirmation, quality time, acts of service, tangible gifts, and physical touch.

I first read Chapman's book, *The 5 Love Languages: The Secret to Love That Lasts*, more than twenty years ago. I don't believe it is overreaching to say it changed my life. I discovered that my primary love language is words of affirmation. I enjoy the other four ways of receiving love, but I am most deeply affected by hearing positive words of support.

Knowing this, my daughter invited people to write me notes for my fiftieth birthday. During the party she planned for me, friends and family members who wanted to speak publicly stood up and shared memories of our times together and what knowing me had meant to them. At the end of the evening, my daughter gave me a box filled with their notes. I felt incredibly loved.

I managed a statewide trade association that was led by a board of directors. The board set the policies and agenda of the organization, and my staff and I implemented them. I believe so much in the value of showing love to people in the way they are most receptive to that I wanted to bring the concept into my work life. It went over well with my staff of three women, but it was a bit awkward with my board members. As part of a leadership training program, I asked board members to take the free love languages assessment online, and then we talked about everyone's results and how we could use that information to better work together. I acknowledged that talking about love languages might seem touchy-feely and uncomfortable for some. Several agreed. Most, but not all, were men. I still believed in the concept, so I searched for something similar to use in the workplace. I found *The 5 Languages of Appreciation in the Workplace* written by Chapman and Dr. Paul White.

In the preface to the book, Chapman said that after the love languages book had sold several million copies and had been translated into forty languages, he started getting testimonies from people sharing how they had adapted the principles to the workplace, sometimes calling them appreciation languages instead of love languages. These individuals encouraged him to write a book on the languages of appreciation and the impact those languages can have on employee satisfaction and increased productivity. Chapman partnered with White, who had extensive experience working closely with leaders of organizations, to develop the book.

The foundational principle of the languages of appreciation is that when individuals feel appreciated and valued in the workplace, they show increased engagement, are less likely to quit, exhibit improved customer service, and gain a deeper sense of purpose. Research published in *Europe's Journal of Psychology* confirmed that appreciation is relevant for both job satisfaction and dedication, no matter how stressful things get at work.

The research indicated receiving appreciation from friends and family is more effective in relieving employee stress. That does not, however, negate the necessity of supervisors and colleagues showing one another their appreciation. Supervisors, customers/clients, and colleagues should all express appreciation on a regular basis.

What Are the Five Languages?

Here is a brief overview of each of the five languages of appreciation:

1. **Acts of Service** : When others reach out to help. There are numerous ways to show people through service that you appreciate them. Consider these things before reaching out to help:

- Make sure your own responsibilities are covered before volunteering to help others.

- Ask before you help.

- Have a cheerful attitude.

- Do it their way.

- Complete what you start.

2. **Tangible Gifts**: Giving meaningful gifts. This is not the same as raises and bonuses. Give gifts primarily to those who appreciate them and make sure to personalize the gift, so it is truly appreciated. Consider these examples:

- Tickets to a sporting event

- Gift cards to restaurants

- Tickets to cultural events

- Small vacations/retreats

- Gift certificates for services

- Gift cards to their favorite stores

- Food treats

3. **Words of Affirmation:** Words are used to communicate positive messages—verbally affirming a positive characteristic about a person. Some personal aspects you can affirm are accomplishments, character traits, and positive personality traits. Use your head, though, and don't say something someone might be offended by or even consider sexual

harassment. When one of my bosses resigned to move on to new opportunities, a guy told her it was too bad she was leaving. "No one else fills out a pantsuit like you do," he said. Completely inappropriate!

- You can appropriately use words of affirmation in a variety of ways:

- Private, one-on-one conversations

- Praise in front of others

- Written affirmations

- Public affirmations

4. **Quality Time**: Giving a person your focused attention. As with words of affirmation, quality time has various dialects, including quality conversations, shared experiences, small-group dialogues, and physical proximity with coworkers in accomplishing projects.

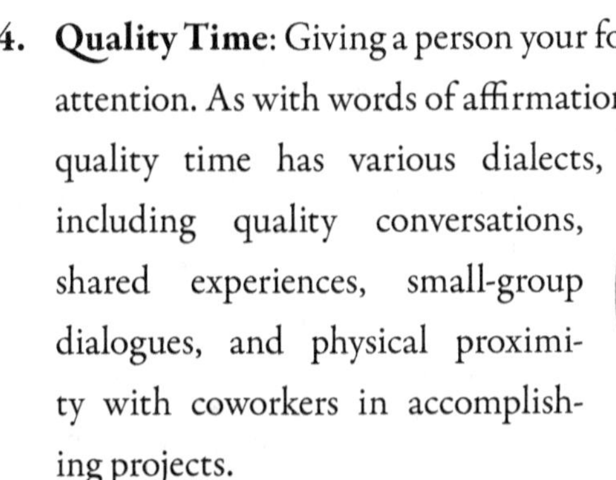

5. **Physical Touch**: There are limited situations where touch is appropriate in the workplace, and few people identify it as their primary language of appreciation. It is still included in discussions, however, because appropriate touch has potential benefits. Before you explore any of those benefits, get to know the culture of your organization. Read the room, and observe how your colleagues interact. Take time to build relationships with people before you engage in any kind of physical touch. Some organizational

cultures are very formal, and only a handshake would be appropriate. Other cultures act more like family. When I worked for the Realtor association, I attended numerous meetings every year. Hugs were the normal way to greet one another, but hugs are not appropriate in every environment. Here are a few examples of appropriate touch in the workplace:

- A firm handshake

- High fives

- Fist bumps

- A pat on the back

An assessment called the Motivating by Appreciation (MBA) Inventory can help you identify your primary appreciation language and your least needed appreciation lan-

guage and your least needed appreciation language. I'll share more about it later in this chapter. For now, just know that the five languages of appreciation in the workplace are the same as the five love languages. However, the two assessments do not necessarily generate the same results. You can't take the free love languages assessment and simply transfer the results to your work life. I tried it and it doesn't work. The questions in each assessment are geared toward different scenarios. In the love languages inventory, subjects are asked to consider their preferences in their personal relationships, such as with a romantic partner, close friend, or family member. The appreciation languages inventory asks questions directly related to the workplace and professional relationships.

My primary love and appreciation languages are the same, but my secondary languages are different. In my personal life, my secondary love language is quality time. I soak up time spent with those I love, even if it's just being in the same room with them and not talking. At work, though, my secondary language of appreciation is acts of service. I am focused on productivity in the workplace, so I want something different from the people with whom I work than I do from my kids, siblings, or friends.

This difference in what we respond to best in personal and professional relationships is why the most significant difference between the two results is with physical touch. I'm sure you can guess why. For these reasons, I recommend you take the MBA Inventory as part of the getting-to-know-yourself process.

Chapman and White developed the MBA Inventory after years of research, studies, and personal experience with clients and patients. You can take the MBA Inventory online at https://www.appreciationatwork.com. Choose from the basic inventory; the expanded inventory for a general work setting; the expanded inventory for remote/long-distance workers; or the medical, military, ministry/nonprofit, school, or government-specific inventories. You will receive a report that shows your primary and secondary languages and your least preferred language.

So how does this information help you get a job and excel in the workplace? The more you know about yourself, the better you can market yourself. When you know your primary language of appreciation, you have a handle on one element of what can either demotivate or motivate you. Learn about the five languages and practice "speaking" them with friends, family, and colleagues. Share your appreciation language with your friends and family and ask them to show you appreciation in this language. If you end up at a company that embraces the practice of showing employees authentic appreciation, you'll be ready to join in. If your new employers are unfamiliar with the program, you could be the one to introduce it to the organization. The closing sentence of *The 5 Languages of Appreciation* says, "By effectively communicating appreciation and encouragement to others, you can be the impetus that creates a more positive work environment for yourself and those around you."

Now, when you start to feel discouraged, you have enough information about your personality type, strengths, and appreciation language to practice self-leadership. Instead of running out of gas and acting like a jerk at work, you are armed with the knowledge to lead yourself away from feelings of discouragement. Take what you have learned about yourself to coach yourself into a refreshed, motivational attitude.

How Am I Doing? Checklist for Success

- ☐ I have taken the 5 Languages of Appreciation Assessment (https://mbainventory.com).

- ☐ My primary language of appreciation is ________________________
  ____

- ☐ My secondary language of appreciation is ____________________
  ____

- ☐ My least preferred language of appreciation is ______________
  ____

- ☐ How can knowing my language of appreciation help me excel in the workplace? ____
  ____

- ☐ How can my knowledge of appreciation languages in general help me excel in the workplace? __________________________________
  ____
  ____

- ☐ How does not receiving appreciation in my preferred language affect my job performance and drop me on the scale from saint to jerk? _____
  ____
  ____

- ☐ How can I positively counteract my own negative reactions to a lack of appreciation in the workplace? ______________________
  ____
  ____

SECTION TWO:
FIRST IMPRESSIONS

You have only one chance to make a good first impression. Amy White, a regional director of Adecco, the staffing agency, has been in the hiring business for more than thirty years. She told me the biggest issue she sees when trying to help people find employment is that they don't know how to market themselves. In the previous section, you learned many valuable things that will help you market yourself to potential employers. Now that you know *what* you're marketing, read on to learn *how* to market yourself.

Your primary marketing materials are your résumé and cover letter. These documents are the first things hiring managers see. They have the greatest impact on the hiring manager's first impression of you. Your second marketing piece is your voice. How you answer the phone, both in person and through voicemail, makes another impression. This interaction is called a phone screening. It is your second chance to make a good impression. If you market yourself well with the résumé and phone screening, you get a third chance to impress at an interview. The interview is an audition for the part of an employee. The interviewer(s) wants to see if you are as good as you sounded in your résumé and on the phone and if you have the qualities they are looking for in an employee. The interview is your last chance to effectively market yourself. This is the sales pitch. You want to make the product (you) so enticing they can't wait to buy (offer you the job). The following chapters will help you develop a professional marketing plan.

As you read the next four chapters, you may feel overwhelmed by the details of putting together a personal marketing campaign. I'm not going to lie. Job hunting is a lot of work. It is time-consuming as well as occasionally mentally and emotionally exhausting. But remember: Looking for a job **is** your job. Do it well, and you'll get that promotion from job seeker to employee.

4. Your Personal Appearance

We have all heard the old saying, "Don't judge a book by its cover." This well-meaning statement is intended to encourage people to avoid forming opinions about others based solely on their clothing, hairstyle, or other outward appearances. But it's only human nature to make snap judgments about people based on the briefest of encounters. Unconscious biases, a topic you'll read more about in Chapter 5, are involuntary judgments we all make countless times a day. They are reflexively triggered by our instincts and are usually informed by our personal experiences and backgrounds. One of the most common is the beauty bias, the tendency to assume the most attractive person is also the most successful. This bias is, of course, untrue. Beauty is subjective; not everyone finds the same people attractive or the same people homely. This bias is detrimental in many ways, including being worrisome for people interviewing for a job. If the person(s) responsible for interviewing candidates falls for this tendency to judge a book (interviewee) by its cover (outward appearance), a deserving candidate could get passed over. You and I know that how you look has nothing to do with how well you do your job, but the bias exists, so let's talk about what you can do to mitigate it while you look for a job. You can't control the biases of others, but you can do your best to present yourself well and make a good impression with your physical appearance.

People joke about turning into their parents. I became my Aunt Beth. Nearly thirty years ago, when she was around the age I am now, she owned a restaurant in my hometown. I have a clear memory of attending my cousin's baby shower in the private dining room at the back of the restaurant. This was the same wood-paneled room with icy blue and soft pink decor where all of our family events took place.

Beth was frustrated about staff turnover. She had just fired one employee and hired two more. She complained about how job seekers looked when they came into the restaurant to apply. She disparaged everything from hairstyles to piercings, tattoos, and ripped jeans (yes, those were already a thing in the early 1990s). I nodded and half-listened as she continued her tirade until she said, "What these young people today need to understand is that it's the people my age doing the hiring. They need to dress to impress me, not their friends."

She had my full attention. Should people have to change who they are to please a boss? Something inside me railed against the idea. What about personal style and personal expression? Wasn't my aunt being terribly narrow-minded? Wasn't she acknowledging a bias against people who looked different than she and her fellow baby boomers did?

I have had three decades to ponder these questions.

Should You Change Who You Are to Please a Boss?

It was naive of me to equate outward appearance with who a person is inside. All employers have a dress code. Many industries require uniforms. Who a person is at their core does not transform each time they change their outfit. Doctors, nurses, firefighters, police officers, UPS drivers, postal service employees, and many more people wear a uniform every day. They voluntarily conform to the industry norm, and their conformity does not change their personalities, values, likes, or dislikes.

Unless you're living off the grid in the wilds of an untamed frontier, you are living in a particular civilization involving societal norms that whole communities agree to embrace. As members of the twenty-first-century global community, we live individual yet similar lives when compared with other eras. Thus, we share multiple common experiences. Traditions and social norms may vary, but overall, we are people living in the technological age. As a whole, we fit a "norm," as did our ancestors from the medieval period or the Victorian era.

Personal Style/Personal Expression

I think this is an area where people really get hung up. We like to express who we see ourselves to be through the way we decorate our bodies. We may do that through hair color and style, clothes, jewelry, tattoos, even a signature scent. It's common to think these outer displays define who we are.

Have you ever gone shopping with a friend who grabs a clothing item, holds it up, and says, "Oh! This is so you!" Your friend means the item looks like something you would wear. Sometimes we agree with their opinion. Other times, we look at the item and wonder if our friend really knows us at all!

Perhaps you've received a gift and thought, "This just isn't me." You don't identify yourself as someone who would like what the gifter chose for you. You don't see yourself in the item.

It's important to have an understanding of what makes us feel most comfortable. It's fine to have a personal style and to express ourselves in our outward appearance. Just don't expect every employer to like what you're expressing.

Rather than changing yourself or changing your personal style to please an employer, consider what type of job best fits your personality and how you choose to outwardly express yourself.

If you're passionate about your luscious beard, you probably don't want to apply for a job that requires you to be clean-shaven. Beards are great, but some jobs, like firefighting, require an airtight seal on face masks. Beards interfere with safety protocols.

If you hate wearing a suit and tie every day, perhaps a job in the legal field isn't for you.

I didn't have enough life experience to fully appreciate what my aunt was trying to express. When she said, "They need to impress me, not their friends," I thought she was being narrow-minded. But now I know she was right. There is a time and a place for everything. She didn't expect staff to change who they were. She didn't expect them to stop expressing themselves. She just wanted them to appear clean, tidy, and professional; and to save overt personal expressions for when they were off her clock.

My daughter-in-law used to work for an employment agency. She had a client who could not understand why he never got sent to what he considered "good jobs." At every job he went to, the manager put him to work far away from any customers or clients. He kept getting grunt-work jobs and was mad about what he perceived as racial discrimination.

One day when he complained to my daughter-in-law, she asked him incredulously, "You mean you really don't know?"

"No," he said. "Why won't anyone give me a chance?"

"Well," she replied, "maybe it has something to do with that 'F%$@ You' tattoo on your upper lip!"

Soapbox Alert: Come on, people! This stuff really isn't that hard. Some forms of personal expression just are not appropriate in the workplace. Here's what I want you to remember about personal expression: *I am not hiring you to express yourself. I'm hiring you to represent me and my business!* Wear whatever you want on your personal time. Go nuts tattooing your body. I don't care. But when you clock into your job, cover up offensive tattoos and conform to the dress code. Upper-lip tattoo guy refused to have his tat removed or to grow a mustache to cover it. It's his right to do as he chooses. It's also an employer's right to refuse to hire him because he doesn't appropriately represent the values of the company.

For my generation and the ones before, a stigma was attached to tattoos. They were not as common as they are now, and they were seldom referred to as body art. All of my kids have tattoos, and at first it was difficult for me to accept. I've been friends with Cody since we were in junior high, and his son and my daughter are equally good friends. One day, the tattoo question arose, and Cody and I tried to explain to our kids why it had taken us a while to let go of our biases.

"It was different when we were kids," I said.

"Yeah," Cody agreed. "The only people who had tattoos when we were growing up were old men who got one when they were stationed overseas, and ex-cons."

"Don't forget the Hells Angels," I helpfully added.

"Right," Cody agreed. "Retired servicemen, ex-cons, and biker gangs."

Those were the environments and societal attitudes in which we were raised. A few old Navy guys with anchors tattooed on their left biceps and bad dudes who wanted to kill you—right or wrong. A far cry from body art.

A 2019 article published in the peer-reviewed academic journal *Equality, Diversity and Inclusion* stated that tattoos have historically been considered part of the American counterculture. Tattoos have, however, gained recognition as a form of self-expression and as part of a growing subculture. The article further stated, "Even though tattooing can be viewed as an artistic self-expression, others, especially older individuals, still view the act of tattooing as deviant behavior and as a rebellion against society at large."

Authors J. L. Flanagan and V. J. Lewis cited studies that analyzed customer perceptions and attitudes toward service workers' visible tattoos; they found that older customers had more unfavorable attitudes toward tattoos than did younger customers. These customers admitted to believing those with tattoos were less honest and less intelligent than those without tattoos. I'm not saying these attitudes are right; I'm just saying that negative attitudes about visible tattoos in the workplace are still prevalent.

Flanagan and Lewis concluded on a positive note, writing, "Visible tattoos are becoming more common in the workplace than ever before; attitudes are shifting, stigmas are changing and acceptance of differences in the workplace dynamics and what is deemed workplace norms are being established." Attitudes might be improving, but change takes time. Instead of copping a jerk-at-work attitude of "screw you, I'll do what I want, and you can just get over it," work for change. You can advocate for change in all disagreeable areas of work culture, not just opinions about tattoos. But while you're professionally advocating, you need to work within the current ways if you want to pay your bills.

Personal Hygiene Is Not Optional

Soapbox Alert: There is no excuse for being a dirty bird. I shouldn't even have to have a section on this, but the things I've seen (and smelled) and the stories I've heard from friends convince me I must address this topic. These are the easiest, cheapest, and most important things you can do to exponentially increase your chances of getting hired and excelling in the workplace:

- Take a shower and don't skip the smelly parts—pits, privates, and feet.

- Use deodorant.

- Wash your hair. Greasy, stringy, stinky hair is gross.

- Take care of your dandruff. We all get flakes occasionally, but when your entire back looks like you've been in a snowstorm and your scaly skin is blanketing the office furniture, it's time to do something about it. Every dollar store sells anti-dandruff shampoo. Dig change from under the couch cushions if you have to.

- Brush your teeth and tongue. Bacteria thrive in the mouth, especially on the crevices and elevations of the tongue. Bacteria cause bad breath. So does coffee. Ever hear of coffee breath? I would never be so evil as to suggest anyone give up coffee, but I will say proper oral care makes everyone happy.

- Trim and clean under your fingernails.

- Trim your nose hairs and use a tissue to wipe away boogers.

- Comb or brush your hair. The unkempt, just-rolled-out-of-bed look is fine if you work where you can wear a cap, but if you're in customer service or a professional industry, keep your hair neat.

- Wash and mend your clothes. Body odor, spills, spots, stains, rips, and tears all need to be eradicated from your wardrobe. A friend told me she used to work with a person who regularly came into the office smelling like cat pee. My friend said it wasn't lingering odors from living in a house with a litter box; the coworker actually had cat urine on her clothes!

- Buy a lint roller and use it. You love your fur babies, but the rest of us don't. Please do your best to leave them at home—including as much of their hair as you can.

- Clean your house. If your house stinks, you stink. Get rid of the lingering odors that follow you to work.

In my experience, people who fail to take care of their personal hygiene fail to respect the cleanliness of the workspace. Those who don't exert the energy to take care of themselves seldom exert the energy to perform well in the workplace. Maybe this is a bias, but it is one held far and wide. Don't let it trip you up.

Does Sexy Work?

I recently met a twenty-one-year-old woman who, during our conversation, said she had a job interview in a few days. I asked what job she was interviewing for, and she said she didn't know.

"But I'm not worried about it," she said. "It's an interview with a man, so I have it in the bag."

"Wait a minute," I said. "Do you mean that because you're a chick interviewing with a man, you think if you dress sexy and act flirty, you'll get the job?"

"Of course!" she replied.

Wow. She's playing right into the concept of "erotic capital," a term defined in a 2018 article published in the scientific journal *Sex Roles* as "the social value one acquires through exploiting one's sexual attractiveness." While this concept can apply to both men and women, it is most prevalent with women. Those who support the concept say women should dress in a sexy manner to get men's attention, which results in boosting their confidence and enhancing their ability to succeed in other roles.

Research shows, however, that sexualized attire negatively affects people's competence ratings, especially for women in supervisory roles. In one study, participants viewed images of a woman dressed to accentuate her sexiness and images of the same woman dressed conservatively. Results indicated that when dressed sexily, the female manager elicited perceptions of lower intelligence and competence. Respondents showed fewer positive emotions (happiness, admiration, contentment, comfortableness, supportiveness, and respect) and more negative emotions (irritation, frustration, disgust, shame, and humiliation).

Both men and women report negative perceptions of women who dress to accentuate their sexiness in the workplace. Ever since Eve threw all women for all time under the bus, women have had to fight for equal rights. We have advanced to a point where we are no longer owned by our fathers, brothers, and husbands. It has only been in my lifetime that an American woman could have a bank account in her own name. Our ancestors fought hard to free us from much of the oppression women suffered for millennia. Many battles have been won, but the war continues.

By playing into the erotic capital concept, women feed the stereotype that the only thing she has to offer society is her body. Both men and women can be objectified, but the issue is predominant with perceptions of women. According to the article in *Sex Roles*, "When an individual objectifies someone, they no longer view the body as part of a person, but rather as an object. Objectification can lead people to make undesirable evaluations about the objectified person." Seems to me that people who set out to get ahead in the workplace by playing the sexy card are more likely to be objectified and receive lower evaluations than they would if they had dressed more conservatively.

If you're not convinced, let's look at some reported numbers. Management consultant Susan Heathfield reported in an article on About.com titled "Why Sexy Isn't Better: How Sexual Behavior Can Submarine Your Career" that women who engaged in sexual behavior and sexy dress earned, on average, $25,000 less than women who did not. Heathfield described sexual behavior as women flirting, provocatively crossing their legs, or leaning over a table to let men look down their shirts. Researchers found that those who reported never using sexualized behavior and dress earned an average of three promotions, while women who had engaged in such behaviors averaged only two promotions. The author concluded with the recommendation that people dress for the job they want to have next. She wrote, "Decision makers will appreciate your efforts to dress professionally."

Another study by Tulane University researchers found that women who "send flirtatious e-mail, wear short skirts, or massage a man's shoulders at work win fewer pay raises and promotions."

I know you've heard of the glass ceiling. When Kamala Harris was sworn in as the first female vice president of the United States, memes flooded social media channels proclaiming, "This is the sound of the glass breaking!"

In a 2015 article titled "Unbuttoned: The Interaction Between Provocativeness of Female Work Attire and Occupational Status," researchers contended that women face complex choices when dressing for work.

They cited several studies that indicate women have to work harder to create a good impression in the workplace. The authors reported that studies show wearing sexualized clothing, regardless of occupation, correlates to being "judged more harshly, and evokes more sexualized judgments by mixed gender samples."

The authors also stated that their findings support earlier studies that found dressing sexily generates negative stereotypical reactions of professional competence in the workplace. The higher a woman is in leadership, the more negatively she is perceived for dressing provocatively. So, if you hope to rise far enough to break the glass ceiling at your job, or in your industry, gettin' your sexy on is not going to get you there.

Understanding Proper Business Attire

When you read an employee handbook or the registration materials for a convention or conference, you might find a statement about how employees and attendees are expected to dress. It might say "business casual" or "business formal." What do these descriptions mean?

Let's start with the most dressed-up category and work our way down.

- **Business Formal**: This is not to be confused with formal dress. Formal is what you'd wear to prom—guys in tuxes, girls in gowns. Business formal is a step down from that—full dark suit (usually black) and a conservative tie for men and a nice dress for women. This level of dress is common for more formal awards ceremonies and installation banquets, cocktail receptions, and holiday parties. It's a good time to get dressed up in a professional setting.

- **Business or Business Professional**: This used to be the norm in business. It includes a suit and tie for men and a dress or skirted suit for women. You may see more color variation in business professional suits. Brighter shirts and colorful ties or jewelry are also common in this category. If you ever watched the television series *Bones*, you may have noticed the character FBI Special Agent Seely Booth wore a conservative suit and tie to work every day, but personalized his look with fun, unique socks. You see this level of dress quite often in the legal field and politics; or worn by sales, account, and pharmaceutical representatives. A step down from suits, but still considered business professional are slacks and a collared shirt or sweater for men, and dresses or slacks and blouses or sweaters for women. Closed-toe dress shoes or boots for both men and women are the norm for this category.

- **Business Casual**: This category of dress has become the norm in most workplaces. It is also the most confusing. There is a lot more leeway in this category and therefore a lot more room for error. One survey done by human resources expert and author Susan Heathfield showed that while 56 percent of employees prefer a more relaxed dress code, 41 percent of them admitted to sometimes feeling unsure about whether an item of clothing was appropriate for the office. A survey of senior managers found that the most frequent dress code violations were dressing too casually (47 percent) and displaying too much skin (32 percent). It's better to dress too formally than too casually. I know I see a difference in how I behave based on how I'm dressed. I've also seen this in my coworkers and staff. Research has shown that, in an office setting, the more casually a person dresses, the lower their productivity. In their article in *Human Resource Development Quarterly*, Joy V. Peluchette and Katherine Karl wrote that what people wear to work has a "substantial impact on how one operates within a work-defined role." The authors also said studies show that both men and women report that the "appropriateness of their clothing affected the quality of their performance and their mood in the workplace." Casual Friday is where I've seen the most abuse of a relaxed dress code. I used to tell my staff that a good rule of thumb was that if they would wear it to clean the gutters or scrub toilets, it was too casual for the office. In "What is Business Casual Attire? Dos and Don'ts of Dressing Down for Business" Alison Doyle wrote, "Remember the 'business' part of business casual and leave your old comfortable clothes at home." Over the years I've had many people ask me if jeans are appropriate for business casual wear. The short answer is no. The long answer was brilliantly illustrated to my cousin when she interviewed for a position at our local community college. The person interviewing her said dress was business casual. My cousin asked if nice denim (jeans with a darker wash and no rips) was acceptable. The interviewer said no because they wanted the staff to differentiate themselves from students. Most students today wear jeans, shorts, sweatpants, and the like to classes. The college's dress code was designed to set the employees apart from the students.

- **Casual**: This final style is not usually worn in the workplace unless you're in an industry that Mike Rowe would consider a "dirty job." My son-in-law is an industrial electrician. He wears fire-retardant jeans (FRs), steel-toed boots, and hoodies. By the time he gets home after a twelve-hour day, he is filthy dirty. Casual is the appropriate attire for his job but not for mine. His mom (my daughter's mother-in-law) is the bookkeeper for a welding shop. Jeans and T-shirts are fine for her to wear in the office. It all depends on the type of business and the wishes of the boss, but in most cases, you would dress casually for an office-type job only during inventory or when attending a company picnic.

Closing Thoughts on Workplace Attire

If you're ever in doubt about what to wear at work, read the dress code section in the employee handbook. Observe what your manager wears. If you really aren't sure about something, leave it at home. Wear what you know is acceptable.

COVID protocols have changed the way people look for jobs, but if you find yourself cold-calling on businesses to ask whether they have any job openings, dress appropriately. When I worked in a women's clothing store, a girl came in holding her boyfriend's hand. She was wearing a tight white tank top and shorts that were so short her butt cheeks were clearly visible. Her boyfriend held a stack of papers in his other hand. She asked if we were hiring as her boyfriend held out what I assumed was her résumé. We weren't hiring, but she would not have been considered anyway for two reasons. The first is that she came in with her boyfriend. That is completely unprofessional and leaves employers wondering if the person is independent and confident enough to do a job on their own. The second reason is the way she was dressed. It was not appropriate for inquiring about ANY job. If you want to apply at a retail store, I recommend going to the store first and noticing how their employees are dressed. Go back on another day, dressed similarly to the employees, to ask about filling out an application.

Dress for the job you want. When my daughter interviewed for a position at our local ski area, she wore a Columbia sweater with a wool vest and a silk scarf, nice jeans, and warm winter boots. She dressed professionally for an outdoor job while showing she had appropriate cold-weather

"ARE YOU HIRING?"

gear and knew how to dress for the conditions. Consider what is standard in the industry in which you're hoping to work and then dress for that industry.

When you get dressed for an interview, dress one step up from what you would wear on a typical day at the new job. Job interviews are one place where dressing a bit too formally is way better than dressing too casually. Again, choose your interview outfit based on the position for which you're applying. If you're interviewing for a server position at Olive Garden, it's unnecessary to wear a suit and tie or a Hillary Clinton pantsuit. On the other hand, don't show up in jeans, tennis shoes, and a T-shirt. Take it up a notch from that: khakis and a collared shirt for men. Women, your choices are vast; just remember everything I've said about dressing sexy or too casually. Wear closed-toe shoes for an interview. It looks more professional. Depending on the job, you may be able to wear sandals once you're hired. Some industries do not allow open-toe shoes for safety reasons.

I love bright colors and crazy patterns, but standards indicate that more subdued colors and little or no pattern are preferred for interviews. Don't dress too flashy but do dress in colors that are flattering to your skin tone. My friend Amelia went for a professional position that required business attire for the interview. She knew black washed her out, leaving her looking too pale, so she chose a soft salmon-colored skirt and matching suit jacket. She told me that when she arrived, all of the other candidates were dressed in black. It made her nervous, but she knew she looked her best. They ended up hiring her, and she worked for the company more than ten years.

The main thing to take away from reading this chapter is to be well-groomed and dressed in clean clothes that are not too casual or revealing. Your personal appearance is absolutely vital to your employment success. If you marked "I'm just a super casual person and it doesn't matter what I wear to work; I'm still a hard worker" on the Jerk @ Work Checklist, you now know why that earned you a jerk @ work score, or at least a mildly annoying score. Dress appropriately for the job you want, and you can erase one more checkmark.

How Am I Doing? Checklist for Success

☐ I understand that when I interview for a job, the employer is looking for a person with the skills, talents, and personality to fit into an already established company culture. My appearance is extremely important to my professional success.

☐ I have thought about the type of job I want and know what is expected of one's appearance (e.g., visible tattoos, piercings, dress code) and am willing to make any appropriate accommodations.

☐ I understand there is a time and place for self-expression.

☐ I accept that, when hired, I will represent my new employer. Therefore, some forms of self-expression may be best reserved for outside of work hours.

☐ My main takeaway from this chapter is _______________________

____

____

☐ One aspect of my appearance that I feel very confident about is

____

____

☐ One thing about my appearance I want to improve is ___________

____

____

5. Your Résumé

Six seconds. That's the average amount of time hiring managers spend looking at each résumé—that is, if they even look at it. Some organizations use an applicant tracking system (ATS), a software system designed to scan and store résumés. The software ranks applicants based on the number of keywords in the résumé that match the job description input by the employer. Originally, ATS was mostly used by large corporations and Fortune 500 companies. Now, however, smaller companies are experiencing a rise in efficiency through ATS, saving time and costs in their hiring process. My point is you won't know if your résumé is going to be read by a human or put through a software system.

You want to make it through the first round, no matter what. While I don't recommend channeling your inner Elle and printing your résumé on pink perfumed paper, you do want to stand out in a positive way. If you don't get the Elle reference, you can stop now and go watch *Legally Blonde*, but I'd rather you keep reading for tips on how to make your résumé stand out in all the right ways. The alternative is the ever-popular circular file (otherwise known as a trash can).

Every organization has its own hiring process, so I could not possibly cover every scenario. I can, however, tell you what my process was when I was hiring. I received some résumés through the mail, some via email, and some I downloaded from the website of the job search company where I had entered the announcement. I printed out every résumé and started with one pile. I then sat down and did an initial scan of each résumé. I ignored the name and contact information and the objective and went straight to work experience and education. If the résumé showed related experience, I put it in a "keep" pile. If it showed no related experience or transferable skills or I noticed obvious errors, it went into a "discard" pile. This was a VERY quick process. In the second step, I went through the keep pile with more attention. I read the entire résumé and again had a keep and a discard pile. At the end of that step, my keep pile contained the résumés of applicants I intended to call for an interview.

I had three primary reasons for putting a résumé in the discard pile:

1. **Overall sloppiness**: If I received a résumé in the mail or in person and it was crumpled or torn, had something spilled on it, or had a weird odor, it immediately went into the garbage can.

2. **Typos, spelling errors, obvious grammar errors**: I received one résumé where the applicant did not use closing parentheses. Throughout the entire résumé, every phone number had an opening parenthesis but no closing parenthesis. The phone numbers were listed like this: (555 555-1234.

Soapbox Alert: If you cannot put your best foot forward for yourself, I know you won't do it for me. A sloppy résumé tells me you'll be a sloppy employee. Failure to catch mistakes in a document that stands between you and a job tells me that you'll make even more mistakes on my work if I hire you.

3. **No transferable skills related to the open position:** It never mattered to me what industry applicants came from if they had appropriate, transferable skills. I outlined in the job description the specific skills I needed. I expected to see those skills mentioned in the résumé; if they didn't appear, I discarded it.

Before we dive deeper into this chapter, I want to highlight a few key areas for you to remember as you create or evaluate your résumé.

1. **Tailor it:** Customize your résumé to the position for which you are applying. Let's say you have experience working in food services, real estate, the oil field, and insurance sales, and you want to apply for a position in car sales. You will want to highlight all the sales and customer service skills you have acquired from this hodgepodge of work experience. Everything you write in your résumé needs to tell the story of how you would make a great car salesperson

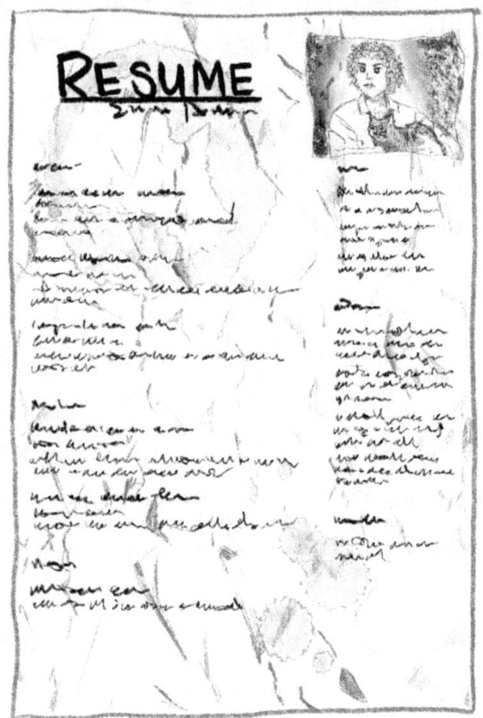

2. **Proofread it:** Have someone else proofread. Proofread. Proofread. Proofread! Did I mention the importance of proofreading? Your résumé should be error-free. According to employment website Career-Builder, 61 percent of recruiters automatically reject a résumé with typos. Similarly, Adecco indicated 43 percent of hiring managers toss résumés because of spelling errors.

3. **Prove it:** If you say you have excellent attention to detail, prove it with an error-free résumé. If you say you have excellent written communication skills, prove it with a well-written résumé and cover letter. If you say you have the education and experience required for the position, prove it by listing relevant work experience, degrees, and certifications.

I want to warn you against some new trends in résumé writing. If you search for résumé tips on Pinterest or Google, you'll find headings like "What Your Résumé Should Look Like in 2022." Most of these examples look like a fancy brochure that contains a photograph of the applicant, links to social media, and cute little graphics to represent telephone, email, and social media channels. These beautifully designed résumés look great, but they are a terrible idea unless you are a graphic designer. If you are one, an eye-catching design might work in your favor, much like a portfolio. If you are not, the design becomes a distraction to the reader; fancy fonts, blocks of color, and photos and graphics will leave hiring managers distracted and overwhelmed. The design also does not influence the computerized ATS. We'll talk more later in this chapter about how to optimize your résumé for the ATS.

My friend Kaitlin, who asked me to use only her first name, is a human resources professional currently working in the manufacturing industry. She said the purpose of a résumé is to help the hiring professional learn the story the applicant has to offer without unconscious bias. Her key piece of advice for job seekers is to skip the photo on your résumé. She said, "People can make split-second decisions on you based on a photo. It is a distraction from your qualifications and experience. It's background noise."

Avoid distractions and potential bias by skipping the cute graphics and photos. Besides, the rejection rate for résumés with a photo rises to 88 percent, according to author Martin Buckland.

Let's Talk Unconscious Bias

There are two types of bias—unconscious and implicit. Both occur automatically as the brain makes quick judgments based on the person's own experiences, situations, and environment. In the 2020 *Kaitiaki Nursing New Zealand* article "Talking About Unconscious Bias," author Jill Clendon defined the two types of bias:

1. Implicit bias refers to the biases people know they have about other people.

2. Unconscious biases are just that—unconscious. The person is not consciously aware of the biases they hold.

Do you remember learning in preschool and kindergarten to put things into categories? Putting the blue toys in this box and red toys in that box, drawing lines on worksheets from one thing to another that is just like it, and playing matching games. This is how your brain was trained to sort and catalog vast amounts of information. Now, as an adult, your brain automatically filters information and subconsciously prioritizes, categorizes, and summarizes your surroundings.

Because the brain automatically lumps similar kinds, forms, colors, and more into single categories, people tend to like what is familiar. According to an article published in *Human Resource Management International Digest,* we tend to like people who look and think like us. The article authors, Himani Oberai and Ila Mehrotra Anand, said some researchers found that repeated exposure to stereotypes and prejudices creates the foundation for unconscious bias. All of us have unconscious bias. The key is to be aware that it exists. We can do this by understanding the seven areas of unconscious bias most prevalent in the workplace. In their article, "Unconscious Bias: Thinking without Thinking," Oberai and Anand described the following types of unconscious bias:

1. **Halo effect**: This describes the tendency to have an overall positive opinion of a person based on a single positive attribute. For example, a hiring manager might assume that because a candidate is good at public speaking, he will also be good at budget analysis.

2. **Affinity bias**: Another term for this is the "like me" bias. This bias is formed when we automatically identify with someone based on a single similarity. For example, a hiring manager could learn what college you graduated from and feel an affinity toward you because he graduated from the same college.

3. **Conformity bias**: This form of bias is caused by peer pressure. You might see this form of bias in a panel interview. One panel member may start to favor or disfavor a candidate because she perceives that the rest of the group is leaning the same way. In this case, the panelists exhibit bias by conforming to groupthink rather than independent thought.

4. **Cloven hoof effect**: This is similar to the halo effect, except in the opposite way. In this form of bias, employers can develop a negative opinion of a person's overall performance based on one negative aspect. For instance, an employee is late only one time, but the boss from then on considers the person unreliable. During the hiring process, a hiring manager might fall for the cloven hoof (also referred to as horns) bias by eliminating a candidate for something trivial like having worked for a company they personally dislike.

5. **Attribution bias**: When we do something good, we own it. When we make a mistake or fail at something, we tend to blame others. We attribute credit or blame to others based on our unconscious biases about them. There is a great scene in an episode of the NBC television show *This Is Us* during a flashback scene when Miguel is offered a job at Lundy, the company from which he would later retire. At the end of the interview, after he has accepted the job, Miguel, who had interviewed as Michael Rivers, tells his new boss that he had submitted two résumés—one as Miguel Rivas and the other as Michael Rivers. The two résumés were identical except for the names. One received a call for an interview; the other did not. Whether it was conscious or not, viewers know the boss had an attribution bias against people of Hispanic heritage.

6. **Beauty bias**: This is the most common form of bias among recruiters. It describes the tendency to think the most physically attractive person will be the most successful employee. Conversely, they could assume an attractive person is too good-looking for the job.

7. **Confirmation bias**: This is the most dangerous of the seven biases because it feeds into negative stereotypes and prejudices. In this situation, the interviewer forms an initial opinion of an applicant and

then subconsciously looks for evidence to prove the opinion right. This might happen when a potential employer makes an assumption about a candidate based on their name or where they went to school. IF they can get past their bias to call the person for an interview, they may steer their questions so they can confirm their initial impression.

Now that you know more about unconscious bias, do you understand why it's a bad idea to include a photo of yourself, your street address, or your memberships in organizations that may indicate your religion, nationality, or other protected information? Your goal is to get past the initial six seconds of résumé review and land an interview. Don't include anything on your résumé that could trigger unconscious bias.

As a general rule, keep your résumé to one page, two at the absolute most. Don't write in complete sentences or use personal pronouns. Write in past tense, rather than present tense since you're giving a history of your skills and experience. Use action verbs and quantitative results. Whatever you do, don't lie or embellish the truth. We'll take a deeper look at each of these recommendations after this list of basic information to include:

1. Name

2. Contact information

3. Work experience

4. Education

5. Related awards, certifications, etc.

6. Related skills

7. Professional references

Let's shift now to take a closer look at each of the standard sections of a résumé.

Contact Information: We no longer live in a world of communicating primarily through postal mail. Today, most communication is done via cell phone calls, texts, and emails. You cannot be discriminated against because of where you live. For these reasons, do not include your home address. It is enough to simply list your name, phone number, and email address.

Soapbox Alert: Make sure you have a professional, marketable email address. Sexy, goofy, vulgar, or punning email monikers are one of the quickest ways to send your résumé to the garbage. Multiple sources state 76 percent of résumés end up in the trash because of an unprofessional email address. Save hotcheeks or darklord for your personal emailing needs and use something simple like your name for a professional email address. Identity theft is always a concern, so resist the urge to use your full name and the last two digits of your birth year. And by the way, even though age discrimination is prohibited, unconscious bias kicks in when we see your email provider is AOL. Yeah, I'm old enough to remember the free AOL discs at the grocery store, but I don't advertise it with my email address. Yahoo and Hotmail are starting to look dated too. If you're looking for a free current email provider, Gmail is the modern standard. Web domains are pretty inexpensive, so about ten years ago, I purchased my name as a domain and set up an email address with it. Feel free to email me at ggreenly@guylagreenly.com. It's crazy how easily impressed people are when they see I have my own domain.

Objective: This is an outdated section of a résumé, so don't include it. You'll still find it on some résumé templates, but I'm telling you I NEVER read them. They are a waste of a hiring manager's time. Everyone is looking for employment with a stable company that utilizes their skills and allows them to contribute to something bigger than themselves. It is fine to skip straight to your work experience, but if you feel the need to put something in place of an objective, consider writing a professional summary.

Professional Summary: If you choose to include this section, focus on the skills and experience you have AND how they benefit the employer. Hiring managers got tired of reading objectives because they all sounded the same and focused on what the applicant wanted. News flash! Hiring managers aren't looking to make your dreams come true. They are looking to find someone who will fill the position and let them get on to the other piles of work on their desks. So don't make the professional summary all about your bad self. Write it in such a way that the hiring manager thinks, "This person is the answer to my needs!"

Skills: This is another section I barely skimmed. Everyone lists "excellent communication skills, able to work independently and in a team, punctual, attention to detail, proficient in Microsoft Office," etc. If you're going to include a skills section, wow me. Take another look at the job description and list the skills you have that match the desired skills outlined in the position advertisement. Popular buzzwords currently are *hard skills* and *soft skills*. Employers look for both sets. Hard skills are easily quantifiable, teachable abilities such as speaking additional languages, operating equipment, or programming computers. These are provable skills, and they can be quantified with a certificate of completion, special licensing, a degree, or a conversation in Spanish (or whatever second language you learned). Soft skills are commonly referred to as people skills or interpersonal skills. Examples include communication, time management, leadership, or customer service. These skills are called soft not because they are less important but because they are harder to demonstrate on a résumé. Because soft skills are subjective, be sure to include specific examples of times you used them in previous positions. Soft skills are often transferable among multiple industries. Where varying industries may have differing hard skill requirements, such as a commercial driver's license or a law degree, virtually all employers are looking for effective communication skills. When you list your skills, think about hard skills specific to the job for which you're applying and soft skills that are transferable from all areas of your life. Adecco's Amy White suggested thinking about what you knew when you started a job and what you know now. "That's your growth, the skills you've developed," she said. When I started working at Casper College Library, I had never managed people (unless you count bossing my little sisters around). In my role as periodicals clerk, I supervised student employees. The next time I applied for a job, I was able to add supervisory skills to my résumé.

Work Experience: This is where you want to list your relevant work experience. You aren't expected to list every job you have ever had. For example, I no longer list Pep's Drive-In or The Bake Haus on my résumé (the local fast-food joint and the café I mentioned in the introduction). Those jobs were too long ago to really matter to a hiring manager today.

On the other hand, if you are just starting out in the workforce, by all means include the fast-food jobs. Hiring personnel like to see you have the experience of showing up on time and following directions. They hope you learned valuable customer service skills, developed interpersonal skills by working on a team, gained the ability to complete tasks in a timely manner, learned to operate the register, and more. When you're starting out, all work experience is valuable and relevant, especially if you have gained transferable skills. You can also include volunteer work and the skills you developed from those experiences.

When my son was in high school, he applied for a lifeguard job at our local aquatics center. He was only sixteen and didn't have a lot of work experience, but he did have several things he could include on his résumé. The two skills he needed to highlight were swimming safety and working with children. Of course, he listed his lifeguard training and certification. He also included that he was on his high school swim team, had completed a basic emergency course, and was currently enrolled in the EMT program at our local college. To show he had experience working with children, he included his experiences volunteering at our local YMCA, assisting his younger sister's basketball coach, serving on mission teams through our church, and volunteering to help with our church's summer vacation Bible school. He ended up working for the aquatics center until he graduated from high school and joined the Army.

NOTE: I know I said before to avoid listing religious affiliations on your résumé. In some cases, such as when you're applying to a faith-based organization or when you have little or no related work experience but you do have volunteer experience, it is better to list them than to ignore them. Just highlight the job duties and accomplishments relevant to the position for which you are applying and leave out overtly "churchy" language.

The professional experience section of your résumé is the most important chapter of the story you tell potential employers. In an article in *Chemical Engineering Progress*, Kimberly Wilson wrote that a résumé should tell a story. "Telling an effective story helps the hiring manager to envision you in the role, even before calling you in for an interview," she said. When you list your previous jobs, don't just list the duties you performed. Wilson recommended describing situations, challenges, problems you solved, and actions you took to create value. Think about how you can quantify your accomplishments, such as "reduced spending 25 percent, " or "increased revenue 30 percent." These types of statements grab attention better and tell a more robust story than "responsible for budget oversight."

It isn't a requirement, but you might consider adding a final bullet in each past work experience description that indicates why you left the position. Employers are always curious about what led you to leave a previous job. They hope you left for growth, new opportunities, more responsibility, more pay, or better benefits, for example. What they don't want is an employee who jumps from job to job because of a short attention span, poor work ethic, or an inability to get along with management and/or coworkers. Save some time in the interview or stop them from tossing your résumé by letting them know why you left. Just make sure your listed reasons are professional and positive. Never trash your former bosses or coworkers, especially on a résumé or in a cover letter! This is a good time to remember the old adage, "If you can't say anything nice, don't say anything at all."

When writing a résumé, do not write in complete sentences or use personal pronouns. Use bullet points and active verbs. Be as concise as possible while giving enough detail to demonstrate you are a perfect fit for the position. The story you want to tell is, "I did all these great things for my previous employers. Let me achieve similar miracles for you."

Education: The "rules" for this section are similar to those for work experience. If you're still in high school, list the name of your high school, the year you started, and your expected graduation date. If you are in college, list your school's name, the year you started, the date you intend to graduate, and your major. Once you have a bachelor's degree or higher, it is unnecessary to list your high school. As I'm writing this book, it has been thirty-five years since I graduated from high school. I have two associate degrees, one bachelor's, one master's, and a doctorate. I no longer include my high school information or my associate degrees on my résumé. If you graduated with honors, such as valedictorian of your high school class or magna cum laude from your university, include that. It really isn't necessary to include your GPA unless you are a recent graduate in a highly competitive market. In that case, a high GPA (3.8 or higher) might catch the human resources professional's eye.

Include any certifications you have earned. Again, when you're just starting out, list everything! Such certifications show initiative and the ability to finish what you start. Once you've been in the workforce for a while, you can start eliminating things that don't directly relate to the job for which you're applying. For example, I no longer include the certificate in newsletter publishing I earned twenty-five years ago. The world of newsletters has drastically changed over the past several decades, so this certificate is no longer relevant. "Dealing with Difficult People" was a popular seminar many employees attended in the 1990s. I have a certificate of completion somewhere, but I don't put it on my résumé anymore. It is still best to have a one-page résumé if at all possible, especially if you have less than ten years of work-related experience. A two-page résumé is acceptable. Three or more pages is a major no-no! Use your discernment to decide what is no longer relevant and delete it. If some certifications or additional training are too old to still be relevant or don't apply to the position you are seeking, leave them off. Definitely omit expired licenses or certifications.

For example, when my son was in high school and applied for the life-guard position, he had an active lifeguard certification. It was current and relevant, so he included it on his résumé. Nearly ten years later, he has let his certification expire, so he deleted it. My sister earned an associate of applied science in cosmetology and held a cosmetology license. When working in the cosmetology field, she included both the degree and the license on her résumé. She is no longer working in the field and has let her license expire. So, if she were to apply for a job today, she would still list the associate degree under education, but she would not include an expired license.

References: There are conflicting opinions about whether references belong on a résumé. Some say leave this section off. According to a 2017 blog post by board certified coach and career strategist Anita Flowers, references take up prime real estate on a document meant to grab an employer's attention in mere seconds. Flowers wrote, "If you make it through the initial screening, employers will ask for references." White, of Adecco, disagrees. The days of stating "references available upon request" at the end of your résumé are over, White said. She prefers to see references on the résumé, so she doesn't have to ask for them later. Include the name, title, phone number, and email address of each reference. Three is the standard number of references. Choose people who can honestly speak about your experience, work performance, and personal character. I know she loves you, but DO NOT list your mom as a reference, even if she has a different last name than yours. The same goes for spouses and significant others. In fact, fathers, siblings, and other close relatives are not ideal references. Unless you worked for one of them in the family business and they truly can give you a professional reference, leave them off.

I once hired a bookkeeper who listed experience keeping books for a small business. She listed her former boss as a reference. When I called, he confirmed she had indeed been employed with him. A few short months later, it was obvious she was in way over her head! She struggled to handle the most basic record-keeping functions. Imagine my surprise when I found out her previous boss was her husband, whose last name she had not taken when they married. Her bookkeeping experience with him had been to pay the bills. She had no experience with purchase orders, invoices, or charts of accounts. Don't exaggerate your skills, experiences, or references. We will find out, and it won't end well for you professionally.

Another tip: Don't include your current bosses unless they already know you are looking for a different job and agree to be listed as a reference. If you don't have any work experience, consider listing teachers, coaches, or the neighbors for whom you babysat or mowed lawns. It is considered polite and professional to ask each person for their permission to use them as a reference, and to confirm the phone number and email address they would like you to include. Some may want to use their professional contact information; others may prefer their personal information.

Social Media Links, Yay or Nay?

While it is true hiring managers will do a basic internet search of your name and check out your social media channels, it's best not to include links to them on your résumé. They add to the clutter that distracts hiring professionals from seeing your relevant skills and education. The only time it is appropriate to include links to social media, other than LinkedIn, is if you are an artist, photographer, graphic designer, or another creator with a portfolio. In that case, the social media link you include should be to a profile solely dedicated to your creations.

Ninety-three percent of recruiters will review your social media profiles as part of their screening process. In an article published on Business 2 Community, Martin Buckland reported that 68 percent of employers will search your Facebook profile. While there are many social media platforms employers might check, every friend I have who hires people says they look up candidates on the most common social media platforms — Facebook, LinkedIn, and Instagram. I know I did. Remember the applicant who never used a closing parenthesis? Everything she wrote on her Facebook page was in lowercase with no punctuation and contained multiple spelling errors and atrocious grammar. Sure, your social media channels are personal, but if you don't have the highest security levels set and any stranger can find your profile and see all of your posts, you deserve whatever judgment others render. Employers want tech-savvy employees with discernment and discretion. Unless you're a public personality, having your personal Facebook page set to public shows me you lack security consciousness, discernment, and discretion. When you're job prospecting, clean up your social media channels.

Both Kaitlin and White told me it is common for employers to conduct background checks and do drug testing. One way hiring professionals do them is by conducting an online search of applicants' names. "We Google someone's name and see what comes up," Kaitlin said. She also said they check free public records for the most up-to-date information about police records and other data.

One applicant surprised a hiring manager, and it takes a lot to do that. The hiring manager had conducted a phone screening and an interview with an applicant. She noticed some red flags related to work history during the interview, so she conducted an additional background check that included a social media check. She found the applicant's Facebook profile, which was completely open. One of his posts stated he was going to "fool these hiring managers with a photo of a white family."

White said, "They don't think we are very smart—that we won't find out things about them."

Kaitlin recommended maintaining a professional outlook on social media posts so that hiring managers don't pick up on anything you don't want them to see. Make your profile private. Google your own name and see what comes up. Ensure you are ready for online scrutiny.

Tips for an ATS-Friendly Résumé

Use of computerized ATS has become the norm for many organizations. Buckland reported that ATS can quickly eliminate résumés and does so at a rate of 75 percent of all applications. Follow the recommendations below so your résumé is elevated to the other 25 percent.

- Save your résumé as yournamejobtitle.doc. A Word document is best. Don't save your document as a PDF because they do not scan well into the software.

- Leave the header and footer blank; the ATS system doesn't read those areas.

- Create your résumé in a standard eight-and-a-half by eleven page size.

- Label your phone number and email address with words, not icons, to help your vital information stand out, for example, Phone: (555) 555-5555 and Email: yourname@gmail.com.

- Include section headings, such as Skills, Work Experience, and Education. This helps the software accurately categorize your information.

- Use an easy-to-scan font such as Arial, Tahoma, Georgia, or Verdana.

- Use as many keywords as possible. Pull keywords directly from the job description.

- Traditionally, we place dates on the left and the name of the company or school on the right. For the benefit of the scanning software, flip the order. Start with the name of the company you worked for, followed by the job title you held and the dates. This format helps the scanning software correctly correlate the information. Example:

- Name of Company   Job Title   2010-2015

The Cover Letter

It may seem backward, but write your cover letter after writing your résumé. When I first started writing scholarly papers in grad school, I tried to write the abstract first because it comes before the rest of the paper. I quickly learned to write the entire paper and then go back and write the abstract. The abstract is basically a summary of the document. How do you summarize what you haven't yet written? It's the same with a cover letter. Write the résumé first, and then write the cover letter.

Jewlsy Mathews, the lead optometrist and person responsible for hiring staff for her optometry practice, said she is more interested in the cover letter than the résumé because it is a "blank canvas for the candidate to showcase themselves." Mathews said applicants could "talk about their wider experiences and how that informs them professionally."

In her research on recruitment selection factors, Katheryn Meagher cited multiple scholars who agreed that the purpose of a cover letter is to demonstrate applicants' writing skills and reveal their personality. According to Meagher, the essential elements of a cover letter are tone, good grammar, and spelling; it should also show how the applicant's education and experience correlate with the job requirements. She surveyed recruiters and found that the following aspects of a cover letter were the most positively noticeable:

- It includes a statement about where the person found out about the job opening.

- Overall, it presents a neat and clean appearance.

- It is specific to the position and not just a generic template.

- It is not an exact repeat of the résumé.

- It is short and concise, and it states why the applicant is a good fit for the position.

Remember, the cover letter is another chapter in the story you are telling potential employers. Make sure it is error-free, including spelling, grammar, and content. Your cover letter, your résumé, and the job for which you are applying should all agree. If they don't, your résumé likely won't go any further.

Neva Bodin, a registered nurse, told me about an application she received. The applicant was seeking a position in the medical field, but his cover letter referenced a job in retail. "And as if that wasn't enough," Bodin said, "he listed attention to detail as one of his skills!" The story he told with his cover letter and résumé and the corresponding job opening was not the story he intended to tell. Bodin immediately discarded his submission, but she will never forget his errors.

Use a professional yet friendly tone. Don't try to sound stuffy or academic. Most people respond best to simple language. If you throw in too many big words and complicated phrases that you wouldn't use in normal conversation, it comes across as though you are insecure and trying too hard to impress. Be yourself but be polite. If there is a gap in your employment, a short sentence in the cover letter is a great way to explain it. If possible, explain how the absence from the workforce helped prepare you for this position.

Keep the letter short. Three paragraphs are enough:

- **Paragraph 1, The introduction:** Tell what position you are applying for, how you heard about it, and why you decided to apply. If you were personally referred, this is where you want to drop that name.

- **Paragraph 2, The Sales Pitch:** Point out the aspects of your employment, education, and personal experiences that make you perfect for the job. Don't just regurgitate what is in your résumé. Pull out new, interesting, and relevant information you weren't able to include in the résumé. Suppose you're applying for a position as a chef at a Cuban restaurant, and you spent a gap year backpacking across Cuba, sampling the local cuisine, and trying your own recipes using traditional Cuban ingredients. The cover letter is the perfect place to share that part of your story.

- **Paragraph 3, The Conclusion:** Just like you did with the concluding paragraph of essays you wrote in school, restate your thesis in one summary sentence. State how you can add value to the organization. Reiterate your interest in the company and thank them for considering your application.

Writing résumés and cover letters is hard, time-consuming work. It's well worth it, though, unless you like being broke. If that's the case, why are you still reading this book? Oh, because your parents are kicking you out of the basement? Then by all means, keep reading! Better yet, put the book down, go write your résumé and cover letter, and then come back and check your work against the checklist below. You got this!

Hey! When you finish your résumé and cover letter, you can erase FOUR checkmarks on the Jerk @ Work Checklist! Look at you making your way toward saint!

How Am I Doing? Checklist for Success

☐ I have a marketable, professional email address.

☐ I have used an easy-to-scan font.

☐ I have left the header and footer blank.

☐ I have used a one-inch margin on an eight-and-a-half by eleven document.

☐ I have included proper headings to organize information.

☐ I have tailored the résumé to the position for which I'm applying.

☐ I have used keywords from the job description.

☐ I have typed the company or educational institution on the left and the dates on the right.

☐ I have included reasons for leaving previous positions. Reasons are professional and positive, not disparaging of past employers or coworkers.

☐ I have included references' names, titles, phone numbers, and email addresses.

☐ Where possible, I have shown quantitative measures of success.

☐ I have included transferable skills, including hard and soft skills.

☐ I have written a clear, concise, targeted cover letter.

☐ If my cover letter and résumé are printed, I used white paper.

☐ I have conducted an online search of my own name and cleaned up any negative references I could.

6. Scheduling the Interview

There is a saying in real estate that the house you live in is not the same as the house you are selling. Real estate agents recommend staging your home to appeal to potential buyers. They suggest eliminating clutter and putting away family photos. Sellers want potential buyers to imagine themselves living in the space. The same principle applies to your phone etiquette during a job search. You want the potential employer to be able to positively imagine you working for them.

First, have a professional-sounding message recorded on your voicemail. There is nothing hiring managers hate more than the prank voicemail. You know the one—the message that leads callers to believe you are live on the other end, followed by the "psych!" moment when you reveal the caller has actually reached voicemail. While this type of greeting might be fun for your friends, it is a massive waste of time and a major annoyance for busy professionals. It is best to have a short, simple voicemail message that identifies you and asks the caller to leave a message. Don't complicate the message. Simply say something like, "You have reached the voicemail of Jane Doe. Please leave a message. Thank you."

Second, answer the phone professionally. "Buddy the Elf. What's your favorite color?" is not an ideal response. Employers assess every interaction with you, including the initial phone call. Save them time by answering the phone with a statement, such as, "Hello, Jane Doe speaking." I respond by simply saying, "This is Guyla." Callers immediately know they have reached the appropriate party.

One of the essential skills I looked for in employees was customer service, particularly via the telephone. When I scheduled applicants for an interview, I called them myself and made a note of how they answered the phone and how well they maintained a conversation. One person I called had a cranky tone to her voice and answered with a sharp, bark-like "HELLO!" When I asked, "Is this Jane Doe?" she maintained her grumpy tone and said, "Yeah." As soon as I identified myself, she completely changed her style and became friendly and accommodating. My interaction with her on the phone left a lasting negative impression and was enough to eliminate her from my list of candidates.

Employers and HR personnel often use the initial phone call as a preliminary mini-interview. During this phone screening, they pay attention to how you answer the phone, how well you answer their questions, what information you either withhold or voluntarily offer, and how confident and prepared you sound.

Finally, be prepared for the phone call. Don't put in your application and then go about life as though you'll never get a call. Keep in mind that you could receive a phone call from a hiring professional at any time. Some companies have HR staff who can call during normal business hours. Others, particularly small-business owners, may do their own hiring. They may call you in the evening after the business has closed for the day, when they can work uninterrupted. Have all of your appointments and commitments entered into the calendar on your phone. That way, no matter where you are when you receive the call, you can confirm a day and time for an interview. While it is OK to tell the caller you need to check your calendar, it is best to take care of it during the call. It saves you and the caller time and shows that you are organized and prepared. Hiring professionals usually have a specific day and block of times set aside for conducting interviews. When they call to ask you to interview, they will either tell you when they want you to come in or give you a range of dates and times from which to choose.

In addition to having an updated calendar, you should know what questions to ask so you are best prepared for the interview. Keep paper and a pen with you so you're ready to make notes. Better yet, write out your questions on a piece of paper and carry them with you in a purse or folded up in your wallet. The caller might voluntarily give you the information you need, but you'll be prepared to ask if they don't.

Confirm Interview Format

- Are you meeting in person, on the phone, or on a videoconference? If the interview is in person, confirm the address. For a phone interview, ask if someone will call you or if you are to initiate the call. If it is a video call, ask when you can expect to receive the link to the call and what provider they use. By having this information ahead of time, you can download the appropriate software and familiarize yourself with the platform.

- Is it a panel interview or a one-on-one interview? In a panel interview, several people who make up an interview committee conduct the interview. Usually, one person leads the interview, but others on the panel participate in asking questions. In some cases, each panel member has a specific list of questions they ask each candidate.

Confirm Contact Information

- Ask for the name, phone number, and email address of a contact person. Emergencies happen. If you get sick, have a family crisis, or break down on the side of the road on your way to the interview, you need to have a person to call. Calling to cancel or reschedule an interview is far more professional than just not showing up. There is also a possibility you could take another job before a scheduled interview. If so, you'll want to call the contact person to let them know you are withdrawing your application.

What If They Email Instead?

You might not receive a phone call inviting you to interview. Instead, you might receive an email. My kids (ages 26, 28, and 29) tell me they RARELY check their email. When you're job searching, make it a habit to check your email every day. Check spam as well, so you don't miss an opportunity. My cousin Kate almost missed an interview request because she hadn't checked her spam for two days. She was relieved to have found the email in time to respond.

- Read the full email carefully. The employer may require tests prior to the interview, such as a typing test or a basic knowledge quiz. Links in the body of the email might refer you to the assessments they want you to take. Follow all instructions and complete any screening tasks you are asked to do.

- When you respond to the email, keep your message short and to the point. Spell-check, reread for clarity, and have someone else proofread it before hitting Send.

Sample List of Questions to Ask When Invited to Schedule an Interview

1. Date and time of interview: _______________________________

2. Format of interview

   ○ In-person

      · Address: _______________________________
        (Is there an office or suite number?)

   ○ Telephone

      · They are calling me.

      · I'm calling them. Phone number: _______________

   ○ Video

      · Platform (Zoom, Skype, Google Hangouts, etc.)

        ____

      · When to expect an email with the link _____________

3. Who is conducting the interview?

   • Name and contact information of person conducting single-person interview: _______________________

   • Number of people in a panel interview: _______________

   • Name of panel chairperson: _______________________

4. Whom do I contact in case of an emergency?

   ____

How Am I Doing? Checklist for Success

☐ I have recorded a short, professional voicemail greeting.

☐ I know how I will answer the phone and, if necessary, have practiced with a friend.

☐ My online calendar is up-to-date.

☐ My email inbox is cleaned out, and I'm ready to receive messages from potential employers.

☐ I know what questions to ask when I receive a call to set up an interview.

☐ I have a paper and pen with me at all times.

☐ Bonus points: I carry a list of questions with me so I can fill in the appropriate information wherever I am when I receive a call to schedule an interview.

Congratulations! If you checked each of these boxes, you can now erase two more checkmarks from the Jerk @ Work Checklist.

7. The Interview

My dad used to tell my teenage self, "There is not enough time in your life to make every mistake, so please learn from mine." I am offering you the same advice. I've made my fair share of mistakes in job interviews, and as an employer, I've seen a lot of mistakes made by others. I have many friends and colleagues with decades of experience interviewing job candidates, and they have shared some doozies with me.

You've put in a lot of hard work on your résumé and followed the previous chapter's tips about scheduling the interview, so don't blow it now! Let's talk dos and don'ts of the interview.

How to Prep for Any Interview

1. Hopefully, you did a bit of research about the company before you applied. If not, now would be an excellent time to learn what you can about what the organization does, whom they serve, what products they sell or services they provide, and more.

2. Review the job description and make notes about how you meet the qualifications they are seeking. Make a list of questions you would like to ask.

Tips for an In-Person Interview

1. Print copies of your résumé and put them in a clean folder or large envelope. The interviewer will most likely have a copy, but it never hurts to be prepared in case a fresh, clean copy is needed. Take one copy for each member of the panel if more than one person is interviewing you.

2. When you're getting ready for the interview, don't go heavy on perfume or cologne! A little bit of that stuff goes a looong way. You also never know when you might meet with a person who has allergies. I am extremely sensitive to smells. I once interviewed a woman who made me think of the old cartoon character Pepe Le Pew. I could almost see the cloud of perfume engulfing her. I had difficulty completing the interview through my watering eyes, itching tongue, and slowly closing airway.

3. Make sure you know the meeting space's location and how to get there. If you are unfamiliar with the area, make a test run. Drive to the site and note how long it took you to get there. Find out where you will need to park and what door you will enter. This practice run will help ease some of your anxiety, save time on the day of the interview, and help you arrive on time.

4. Arrive no more than five minutes early. You'll find conflicting opinions about this on the internet. Some say to arrive fifteen minutes early. I'm telling you right now, that is way too early. Here's what happens when you arrive fifteen to twenty minutes early.

    - You annoy the receptionist, especially if you're chatty.

    - Interviewers often schedule all or many of their interviews on the same day with a fifteen-minute passing period between them. This allows for various contingencies such as an interview going long, the interviewer having time to take a breath or a comfort break, and candidates not passing each other in the reception area.

    - You make yourself more nervous sitting there waiting.

    - Arriving five minutes early is enough to let the potential employer know you are conscientious and prompt.

- If you really must arrive more than five minutes early, sit in your car until ten minutes before your scheduled appointment. This allows five minutes to walk into the building and find the correct office.

5. Greet the receptionist with this simple statement: "Hello, I'm John Doe. I have a three-thirty appointment with Mrs. Smith." You might be tempted, but DO NOT give the receptionist your life story, share the tragic tale of narrowly missing an accident on your way to the interview, or explain why you are so excited to work at this company.

6. Silence your phone. Better yet, turn it off and put it away, or leave it in the car. Whatever you do, don't answer it during the interview. An employee at my local chamber of commerce told me about a person who answered his phone during an interview and casually chatted with the person on the other line as though he had nothing else going on!

How to Prep for a Video Interview

According to White at Adecco, "We are seeing fewer people in person. People need to know how to apply online and interview by Zoom." I don't know if this trend of online interviewing will decrease along with our recovery from the COVID pandemic. I do know, however, that the technology is here to stay, so you need to be prepared for the likely event you will be asked to interview remotely.

1. If your interview is via phone call or videoconference (Zoom, Skype, Google Hangouts, etc.), make sure your phone or computer has a full charge. You'll also want to be sure you have the appropriate software installed for a videoconference.

2. Try the link to the meeting at least thirty minutes before the scheduled interview to ensure your speakers, microphone, and internet are all working. In most cases, you won't be entered into the room until the host starts the meeting. Once you have checked out your hardware, you can disconnect until it's time to join the actual meeting.

3. Dress as you would if you were meeting in person. A strange phenomenon has developed where people seem to think an online meeting is the equivalent of shopping in Wal-Mart at three a.m. It's a video call; they CAN see you. White said, "We are conducting interviews via Zoom. People aren't dressing for the interview. They look like they just rolled out of bed."

4. Join the videoconference a few minutes before the scheduled interview. It sometimes takes a bit of time for the link to connect and the software to open.

5. Conduct yourself in the video interview just as you would if you were meeting in person.

Avoid These Mistakes

1. Do not wear clothes that cause you to fidget. Wearing clothes that are too tight, too short, or too itchy will keep you messing with your clothes instead of appearing relaxed and focusing on the interview. Women, don't wear low-cut tops or short skirts that reach your midthigh or higher when you are seated. Either you will be uncomfortable and spend your time adjusting your outfit or you will distract those conducting the interview. You may think this sounds sexist, and popular media may have taught you that dressing sexy is the way

to get ahead. But in the real world, especially in the corporate world, there is still a standard of professionalism.

2. Refrain from name-dropping. It doesn't impress anyone. I once interviewed a woman who was new to the community. She tried to impress me with her connections by telling me she had attended meetings with several doctors' wives. She mentioned each one by name, oblivious to the fact I had known these women for decades. Our children attended school together, we attended the same church, and we had traveled together internationally. I was not impressed. I saw her as insecure and unprofessional.

3. Don't try to convince the interviewers of your knowledge by talking down to them or acting like an expert on a basic procedure. As I escorted one candidate for an administrative assistant job to the door at the end of an interview, she tried to position herself as the expert on the copy machine we were passing. She went into detail on how to utilize this basic office machine, as though I had no idea how it functioned. Don't insult my intelligence.

4. When they ask the age-old question, "Why should we hire you?" don't say, "Because I'm awesome." I actually did this at the end of a panel interview for a position as an elementary school secretary. I was in the middle of a soul-crushing divorce and desperate for a job, but I was also insecure and nervous. In the moment, answering with a quip seemed like a way to break the tension, but no one laughed. The six panelists just stared at me. I tried to recover by saying that one of my coping mechanisms was to use humor when I was nervous. They continued to stare. I did not get the job, but I learned a valuable lesson. Humor, used sparingly, is fine in the appropriate context, but read the room and know when to just answer the question they asked without joking.

Questions Interviewers Are Not Legally Allowed to Ask

Remember that unconscious bias we discussed in Chapter 5? Some people, intentionally or unintentionally, have made hiring decisions based on criteria considered discriminatory. The United States government enacted laws to protect people from being denied jobs for discriminatory reasons. As a job seeker, you need to know what employers cannot ask and how to respond if they do. You also need to know so that you don't unwittingly tell them without them asking. According to the US Equal Employment Opportunity Commission, "It is illegal to discriminate against someone because of that person's race, color, religion, sex (including gender identity, sexual orientation, and pregnancy), national origin, age, disability or genetic information." The interviewer cannot ask you any questions related to these protected areas. They cannot ask if you are married, have children, attend church, or have any disabilities. They can ask questions about your ability to perform the job duties, availability for travel, and so on. If you think you're being asked an illegal question, take a minute to think about the intent behind the inquiry. Perhaps they asked if you have adequate childcare. It is illegal to ask about your family status, such as marriage and kids. The intent behind the question may be to determine if you are available to work nights and weekends or to travel. Therefore, you might respond with a simple statement about your work availability. If you are asked an illegal question, either answer in a way that rephrases their question to one that is acceptable or politely decline to answer.

Here are a few inappropriate questions an interviewer might ask and suggestions for how to answer.

1. *Are you married?* It is illegal to ask this question because it reveals your marital status and possibly your sexual orientation. You may decline to answer by stating that your marital status does not affect your performance on the job. Employers also are not allowed to ask about your spouse's job or salary. If they do ask, you can simply say your spouse's position does not interfere with your ability to perform the job's duties. A common question in towns with a military base is, "Is your spouse in the military?" They can't ask you this. An employer may be afraid a military spouse is more likely to quit than a civilian spouse. This isn't necessarily true. Employers cannot discriminate against military spouses.

2. *Have you ever been arrested?* Employers cannot ask about your arrest record. They can, however, ask if you have ever been convicted of a crime. Therefore, you can simply say that you have not been convicted

of a crime. Unless you have. In that case, tell them what you were convicted of, and that you have paid your debt to society, learned your lesson, and made positive changes in your life.

3. *What religious holidays do you celebrate?* Unless you are applying for a job at a church, which has a legal exception, your spiritual beliefs have no relevance to your ability to perform the job. They can ask if you are available to work weekends, but they cannot ask about your religion.

4. *Do you have children?* You cannot be denied a job because you have children or plan to have kids. The most common reason unwitting interviewers ask this question is because they are trying to determine if you can work certain hours or days, or if you are available to travel as the position requires. If anyone asks whether you have children, you can phrase your answer to meet the intent of the question. You might say something like, "I am able to travel as necessary and work the days and hours that the job requires."

5. *What country are you from, is English your first language,* or *where were you born?* Employers cannot ask about your nationality, but they can ask if you are authorized to work in this country. If they do ask one of these questions, simply tell them you are authorized to work in this country.

6. *What type of discharge did you receive from the military?* Whether you were honorably or dishonorably discharged is not an appropriate question. However, they can ask what relevant education, training, or work experience you received in the military. If they ask what type of discharge you received, you can answer with any relevant training and experience you garnered during your service.

7. *How tall are you, how much do you weigh,* or *do you have any disabilities?* Employers can ask specific job-related questions such as, "This position requires a lot of standing. Are you able to do that comfortably?" If they ask you anything specific about your physical or mental well-being, you may choose to say something like, "I am confident I am able to handle the requirements of the position."

8. *How old are you, when did you graduate,* or *what is your date of birth?* If a job requires the applicant to be of a certain age, such as for serving alcohol, the interviewer can ask that proof of age be provided upon hiring. Interviewers cannot, however, directly ask your age.

There are many ways someone might ask illegal questions, so I cannot address all of them. The important thing is to be aware of the protected classes and know what interviewers can and cannot ask. By knowing ahead of time what these areas are, you can develop a plan for handling the situation if it arises.

Answering the Most Commonly Asked Interview Questions

There are several questions that are asked in nearly every job interview. You would do well to take notice of them and think ahead to how you will answer. Keep your responses brief, and don't memorize your answers.

1. **Tell me about yourself**: "Tell me about yourself" is a popular opening question, an icebreaker. Do not launch into your life story! Don't give them information on the questions they are not allowed to ask, and do not go on and on and on. My millennial friend with a human resources master's degree says you should give a short overview of your work experience and professional goals and always represent yourself in the best light. It is not uncommon for candidates to ram-

ble on with a long, generic answer. They might rehash their résumé, or volunteer answers to questions interviewers aren't allowed to ask. According to Alison Doyle, job search expert, founder of CareerTool-Belt.com, and blogger with thebalancecaareers.com, interviewers are looking for evidence that you're qualified to do the work and that you'll fit in with the team and company culture. Craft your answer to help you establish a rapport with your interviewer. Keep your answer engaging but brief.

2. **Why do you want this position?:** "Because I'm broke" or "I need health insurance" are not great answers. In fact, they are the quickest way to shut down the interview and guarantee you don't get the job. Hiring managers are trying to determine whether candidates share company values and are committed to seeing themselves succeed in the role for which they're interviewing. Consider how you can connect your professional goals to the organization's.

3. **Where do you see yourself in five years?:** Don't tell your interviewer that you really haven't thought that far ahead. It may have been true before you read this chapter, but now you know that you need to think about it and have an answer prepared. Hiring managers want to know if you see the position as a logical next step for you, and if you'll stick around long enough for them to see a return on their investment of onboarding and training expenses.

4. **What's your greatest weakness?:** Anisa Purbasari Horton and her team at Fast Company reached out to recruiters and hiring managers to find out the worst answers they've received to this question. Horton reported that hiring managers are irritated by candidates who give answers "cloaking their weaknesses as strengths, such as 'I'm a perfectionist' or 'I work too hard.'" I dedicated an entire chapter to

identifying your strengths and why you should focus on them instead of weaknesses. You might wonder, then, why employers ask candidates in interviews to tell them about their greatest weakness. Possibly because they aren't woke to positive psychology and the industry's commitment to concentrate on strengths rather than weaknesses. More likely, though, it's because your answer is one way they can evaluate your self-awareness. An article on Indeed.com titled "Interview Questions: What Are Your Greatest Weaknesses?" said the key to answering this question is to acknowledge that everyone has flaws. The hiring manager wants to see that you are able to assess your current talents and pinpoint areas where you need to improve. According to the article, "Hiring managers are looking for two main insights: your weakness and the steps you're taking to improve." The unnamed author encouraged candidates to prepare a skill-based answer to the question, making the following recommendations for planning how you answer:

- Customize your weakness to the job for which you're applying.

- Choose a skills-based weakness and show concrete steps you're taking to develop that particular skill.

- If you choose to share about a character trait weakness, avoid an example that gives the impression you're unable to collaborate with coworkers or accept constructive criticism.

- Stay positive and respond with an optimistic tone.

- Be prepared. Having an original and thoughtful response shows the hiring manager that you're taking the interview and your career seriously.

- Answer truthfully. A sincere response shows you value honesty.

- Include specific details. Dive deep into your experiences to describe how you've overcome a pertinent obstacle or challenging situation.

Questions to Ask at the End of an Interview

Most interviews end with the interviewer asking applicants if they have any questions. Horton asserted that the "consensus among hiring managers is that lack of questions translates to a lack of interest." She recommended having at least two or three questions prepared. This is when you would want to ask the questions you wrote out during your preparation for the interview and any questions that arose during it.

Here are some sample questions for you to consider if they haven't already been asked:

1. How would you describe the company culture?

2. Can you elaborate on the day-to-day responsibilities this job entails?

3. What does the ideal candidate for this role look like?

4. How have people previously succeeded in this role?

5. How are your employees evaluated?

6. What are some of the challenges you've seen people in this role encounter?

7. Is there anything in my résumé that concerns you?

8. Have I answered all of your questions?

9. Is there anything else I can provide to help you with your decision?

10. What is your timeline for making a decision about the position?

11. Can I expect to hear from you either way?

Don't ask obvious questions, and don't ask questions to which you should already know the answers. Here are some questions to avoid:

1. What exactly does your company do? This is something you should already know. You should have researched the company before applying and certainly before interviewing. Asking this question shows you are lazy and uninterested in the job.

2. Are you going to check my Facebook? This is a dumb question because, yes, most employers will check. Also, by asking, you are implying you have something you're afraid an employer will discover. If the interviewer hadn't planned to check your Facebook, he sure will now!

3. Will I have to work nights or weekends? Can I work from home? Is it OK if I come in a little later? All of these questions sound like you're trying to find the easy way out of hard work and expect special treatment. Specific questions about scheduling are best discussed when and if you are offered the job. Individualized questions such as the ability to work from home are best asked after you have proven yourself a worthy employee capable of self-managing.

4. When can I take a vacation? Asking about time off before you've been offered the position implies you are not a committed worker. It is, however, appropriate to mention if you already have any major trips coming up that might affect the employer's decision. This helps the employer decide if they can work around those commitments and saves them from being blindsided if they offer you the position.

When I interviewed for the executive assistant position at the trade association I've previously mentioned, I told the employer I was already scheduled to go on a two-week trip to Africa. She went ahead and hired me, and when it came time for the trip three months later, I took the time off without pay since I was not yet eligible for vacation. I felt horrible fifteen years later when I forgot to advise my son to mention his upcoming trip to Africa in an interview. They didn't ask about upcoming events, and he didn't give it a thought during the interview. They hired him, and when the HR employee helped him fill out his initial paperwork and explained the time-off policies, he suddenly remembered and blurted it out. She was not impressed and informed him the appropriate time to mention the trip would have been during the interview. She then contacted his immediate supervisor and asked him to explain the situation. She said since the trip was with a charitable organization, they would still hire him and he could take the time off without pay and they were choosing to trust he would not blindside them like that in the future. He promised he would work hard for them before and after the trip, but he felt sick about the incident for quite a while afterward.

5. What are the company perks (or benefits)? This question is best saved for after you have been offered the position.

The primary purpose of an interview is for the hiring manager or employer to decide whether you are qualified for the position and whether you will be a good fit for the position and the company. It is also an opportunity for you to learn more about the expectations of the position, and if you believe you're a good fit for the position and the company. We'll talk more in the next chapter about what to do when you are offered the job.

A Note About Body Language

I grew up humming along with a 1983 stalkerish rock song by The Police promising to always be watching. Much like the ex-girlfriend featured in that '80s classic, every move you make from the moment you walk into the interview to when you walk out will be watched. Those conducting interviews notice everything about you. Author Martin Buckland collected a list of statistics proving just how important body language is. In shockingly high numbers, 2,000 surveyed bosses indicated several non-verbal mistakes that cause them to eliminate candidates:

- 67 percent said failure to make eye contact would kick you out of the running.

- 55 percent said the way the candidate walks through the door influences their opinion.

- 38 percent agreed they look for an attitude of overall confidence.

- 38 percent said the lack of a smile puts a frown on their faces.

- 33 percent are turned off by bad posture.

- 26 percent pass on candidates with a weak handshake.

- 21 percent don't take kindly to candidates crossing their arms over their chests during the interview.

Job interviews are nerve-racking! There is no way around that, but you can lessen the pain by being prepared. If you're not sure what language your body is speaking, try practicing with a friend and recording yourself when you walk into a room, shake hands, sit down, stand back up, and walk out. Watch the footage and take note of your posture. Are you slouching or standing up straight? Did you look your friend in the eye and smile as you offered a firm handshake? Did you slump down in the chair and sprawl out your legs like you were preparing to watch a movie, or did you sit up straight? Did you cross your arms across your chest or sit with your hands in your lap? You might find it quite uncomfortable to watch yourself, but you'll learn a lot about how others see you if you try it.

Whether we realize it or not, we all exhibit either power*ful* or power*less* body postures. Research suggests open and expansive body posture is identified as powerful, whereas constricted or submissive body postures nonverbally reflect a lack of power. By recording yourself in a practice interview, watching it, and then correcting any negative body language, you can practice power posing. In a research article in *Frontiers in Psychology,* the authors defined power posing as "the adoption of open and powerful postures." Standing—or sitting—upright with good posture and hands on hips or behind the head are considered high-power poses. Low-power poses are standing or sitting with hunched shoulders and/or arms crossed over the chest.

I don't recommend using the high-power pose described above because that stance is more aggressive than you want for a job interview. Much like Goldilocks, you don't want to be too aggressive or too passive. You're looking for that "just right" posture. Research indicates that a balanced power pose elicits perceptions of competence and admiration while a low-power pose prompts feeling of pity. The research reported in *Frontiers in Psychology* showed that power posing might be used as performance-enhancing preparation for situations such as job interviews, negotiations, and sales pitches. So go ahead, strike a pose—a power pose.

After the Interview Is Over

Send a thank-you note within twenty-four hours after the interview. A handwritten note mailed to the interviewer is best if you really want to stand out. Sometimes interviewers are able to narrow the choice to two candidates and struggle to choose between them. If you send a handwritten note, that may be the gesture that pushes their decision toward you. A second option is to send a follow-up email, which is more immediate but less impressive.

Either way, following up after the interview allows you another opportunity to show your professionalism, keeps your name in front of the interviewer, and shows your eagerness for the job. In her October 2020 blog post, job search expert Alison Doyle said sending a thank-you note is a must. She said, "Sending a thank-you note shows the employer you are polite and professional. It is also a way to remind the employer who you are."

As you write your thank-you note, think of it as another opportunity to sell yourself. Here are a few short tips:

1. Send it as soon as possible. If the interviewer gave you a short timeline for when they hoped to have a decision, send an email for expediency. If they said they would make a decision within a couple of weeks, send a handwritten note in the mail.

2. Keep it short!

3. Sell yourself. Use the note as an opportunity to remind them of something you discussed in the interview or to add new information you forgot to mention.

4. Proofread! Get a friend to read it too.

5. If you email your note, send it in the body of the email. Do not send an attachment.

How Am I Doing? Checklist for Success

☐ I have chosen an appropriate outfit to wear for the interview.

☐ I have printed copies of my résumé and cover letter.

☐ I have confirmed the date, time, and format of the interview.

☐ For an in-person interview, I know how to get to the meeting and how long it will take me to get there.

☐ If it is a telephone or video interview, I have the appropriate technology, a fully charged battery, and charging cords.

☐ I have researched the company and reviewed the job description.

☐ I am familiar with the protected classes and the types of questions employers cannot ask.

☐ I have a plan for handling any inappropriate questions.

☐ I have thought about how I will answer common questions such as "Tell me about yourself," "Why did you apply for this job?" and "Why should we hire you?"

☐ I know interviewers are also likely to ask me about my weaknesses or my greatest weakness. I plan to respond with

- A skills-based weakness _______________________________

- A character trait weakness _____________________________

- The steps I'm taking (or have taken) to improve in this area

  ____

  ____

  ____

☐ I have a list of questions to ask.

☐ I sent a thank-you note.

SECTION THREE:
YOU GOT THE JOB! NOW WHAT?

Congratulations! You wrote a stellar cover letter, nailed the résumé, aced the phone screening, and made a great impression in the interview. They offered you the job, you accepted, and you start work next week. Now what?

First-day jitters are common, but with some preparation, you can ease your nerves and start your new job like a rock star. From planning what you need to take to work with you on the first day, to a frank conversation about the quickest ways to lose your new job, to tips on how to become indispensable to your new employer, you'll find all you need to know to succeed in your new job in this next section. If you scored Jerk @ Work on the opening checklist, this is the section where you will find the majority of the reasons you scored so high on the scale between saint and jerk. You're making great progress cleaning up your act. Keep going! You'll reach saint soon!

8. Preparing for Your First Day

The first day of a new job is both exciting and scary. As you anticipate the day, a million crazy thoughts may race through your head. What if your alarm doesn't go off and you sleep through the first day of work? What if you make a huge mistake or do something that makes you look foolish? What if you dislike your new boss or coworkers, or worse, what if they don't like you?

Don't let fear of failure derail you. You've been successful in the past. Your new employers obviously think you are qualified for the job and have the qualities and personality to fit with their existing team. Author Dean Gurden encouraged readers of his article in *Nursing Standard* to remember that they were hired for a reason and to make a list of their past successes. I've always struggled with math and barely passed high school Algebra II. In fact, I had to take a no-credit math class my senior year of high school to get into college. When I start worrying I will fail at something new, I remind myself that I took college statistics online during the summer session, completed the textbook, AND got an A. If I can succeed in an online statistics class, I can do anything.

What have you done that you never thought you could? Prepare for your first day at a new job by getting your mind right. Go in armed with the confidence you've succeeded in the past, knowing there is no reason to believe you won't succeed again.

Preparation Dos and Don'ts

I've shared some information in this book that some might think is such common sense that it should go without saying. (See the section on hygiene, for example.)

Speaking of sayings, how about this one: "Common sense is a flower that does not grow in everyone's garden." With that in mind, I'm going to give you a list of things to do and not do in the days before and the morning of your first day of work.

- DO purchase any clothing or materials required for the job. For instance, fire-retardant pants, steel-toed boots, gloves, and a hood for a welding job; or a red polo shirt and khaki pants for a position at Target.

- DO get a haircut, trim your beard, trim your nails, and anything else necessary to be well-groomed and feel confident about your appearance.

- DON'T stay out late, get drunk, or do drugs.

- DO get a good night's sleep.

- DO shower or bathe.

- DO dress appropriately for the job (see Chapter 4).

- DON'T wear heavy perfumes, lotions, or colognes (see Chapter 7).

- DO eat a healthy breakfast hearty enough to hold you until you get a break.

- DO arrive a few minutes early.

- DON'T bring a bunch of personal items to decorate an office or put on your desk. It's better to take as little with you as possible on the first day. Get to know the culture, policies, and environment of your new workplace before personalizing your workspace.

- DO take a notebook and pen or some other way of taking notes. There is no way you'll remember everything you're told on the first day.

Expect to Fill Out Paperwork

A quick internet search asking how to prepare for your first day at a new job results in ridiculously basic information. Several Pinterest articles suggested laying out your clothes the night before and packing your bag with a bottle of water, a sweater, and snacks. Because you're now employed, I'm going to assume you are at least fifteen years old and already know how to stay hydrated, warm, and well-fed. I'm not going to remind you to take a sweater. But I am going to remind you to take the important documents necessary to complete your employee onboarding paperwork. It's best if you are prepared and able to complete everything at once.

Here are the new-hire documents you will need to fill out and the personal documents you will need to supply:

1. **Form I-9**: This form is required by the Internal Revenue Service and is used to verify your eligibility to work in the United States. As the employee, you are responsible for filling out the first section and must complete it on your first day of work. The form has three lists of documents that are acceptable. List A establishes both your identity and your eligibility. I'm not going to recreate the entire list of appropriate documents. If you really want to, you can Google *I-9* or *new hire doc-*

uments and download the form. If you just want the highlights, here are the most common documents you are likely to need:

- US Passport

- A so-called "green card"—Permanent Resident Card Or Alien Registration Receipt Card

- If you don't have a passport or a green card, you can use one item from List B to establish your identity and one from List C to establish your eligibility to work.

  - List B includes officially issued ID cards such as these:

    1. Driver's license

    2. Student ID with photo

    3. Voter registration card

    4. US military ID card

    5. Military dependent's ID card

    6. Native American tribal document

  - From List C you can use one of these:

    1. An unrestricted Social Security card

    2. Certified birth certificate

    3. Native American tribal document

2. **W-4**: This federal form must be filled out before you can receive your first paycheck. So yeah, it's a pretty big deal! To fill out this form, you need to know your Social Security number, how you intend to

file taxes (single or married filing separately, married filing jointly, or head of household). You will also need to know how many dependents you want to claim and whether you want any extra withholdings taken out of each check. The form has detailed instructions, but it can still be confusing the first time you fill one out. Some people like to claim the bare minimum so more taxes are taken from their checks and they can get a refund when they file their taxes. Others like to claim as many dependents as legal so they lower the amount of taxes deducted from each paycheck. The choice is yours. I like to get as much of my earned income as possible rather than give the government an interest-free loan of my money. Others like to pay in extra as a form of savings, so they know they will get a refund check later.

3. **State Tax Withholding Form**: If you live in a state that has a state income tax, you'll have to fill this form out before your first paycheck is issued. It is similar to the W-4.

4. **Employer-Specific forms:** The I-9 and W-4 are forms everyone in every job in the United States is required to fill out. Individual employers may require other documents. These are some examples:

    - Employee Information Form—This is for gathering essential information to include in your personnel file, such as an emergency contact.

    - Equal Opportunity Data Form—Companies with 100 or more employees or federal contractors with 50 or more employees are required to have you fill out this form.

    - Direct Deposit Authorization—Some companies pay employees through direct deposit rather than printing paper checks. If this is the case for your new employer, you'll need to sign an authorization form and provide your banking information. The simplest thing to do is bring a deposit slip for either your checking or savings account to work on the first day.

Summary of Documents to Take to Work on the First Day

I just threw a bunch of boring, albeit vitally important, information at you. Allow me to simplify it in a quick summary. Here are the documents you need to take to work on the first day:

- Driver's license

- Social Security card

- Bank deposit slip

See, it really isn't that difficult. This is a good place for me to go on a rant about your Social Security card.

Soapbox Alert: I know a lot of young people who carry this vital document in their wallets at all times. DON'T DO IT! All hackers need to steal your identity is your full name, birthdate, and Social Security number. If you lose your wallet, bad guys will have everything they need to assume your identity, steal all your cash, and open credit cards in your name. It can take years to clean up an identity-theft mess.

So, after you take your Social Security card to your first day on the job, bring it home, and put it in a safe place. I keep mine in a locked fire-safe box along with other important documents such as birth certificates and vehicle titles.

Most companies have a new-hire onboarding process. Filling out the aforementioned paperwork is one part of it. You should also receive a copy of the employee handbook. You'll be expected to read it and sign a statement of receipt. Make sure you read and understand it. The handbook is where you'll find information about work hours, breaks, holidays, vacation, dress code, and other policies you're expected to follow. You'll likely receive a tour of the facilities, be introduced to coworkers, and be shown to your workstation. Do your best to remember names, but don't beat yourself up if you have to ask someone to repeat their name. No one expects you to remember everyone's names all at once.

Training Tips

Once your training begins, take notes and ask questions. Bob Dolan, a career development counselor at Massechusetts Institute of Technology (MIT), reported that a 2018 survey found that employers look for the following competencies:

- Critical
  thinking/problem solving

- Teamwork/collaboration

- Professionalism/work ethic

- Oral and written communication skills

- Leadership

- Digital technology

- Career management

- Global/multicultural fluency

Paying close attention to instruction, taking notes, asking questions, and working hard are concrete behaviors that will exhibit the first four competencies in the list and lead to your success. Obviously, you want to make a good impression. Do your best and manage your expectations. You will make mistakes. You will have a learning curve. Be patient and extend yourself grace.

When you start a new job, full of ideas and enthusiasm to radiate, you will meet the old, burned-out, cynical curmudgeons. Don't let them dim your shine. Dolan advised against letting gossip influence you. "People may talk and try to warn you about a person or situation," he said. "Don't get caught up in these situations, and come to your own conclusions based on your own observations."

Gurden told readers not to make rash judgments about people and to take time to build trust and respect with colleagues. He also said to avoid talking about how things were done differently or better at your old job. Listen more than you talk. Take it all in. Learn everything you can about your new responsibilities, the expectations for performing your job, and the culture of your new organization. Learn your new role, prove your abilities, and gain the trust of your supervisors and colleagues; THEN you can suggest alternative ways of doing things.

First Hundred Days on the Job

Dolan indicated that the first hundred days on the job are the most critical for a successful transition. He outlined four key areas of focus for you.

The first thing you want to do is understand the culture. Amy White agreed, saying, "Find a way to fit into the culture." To do this, Dolan recommended paying attention to how people interact and how things are done. He suggested considering the following:

- Do people collaborate or compete?

- Do people communicate face-to-face or electronically?

- Does management empower employees or micromanage them?

- Are people open and friendly or quiet and businesslike?

- Does the company respect diversity (gender, language, religion, etc.)?

- Are there any other company norms?

The second area of focus Dolan recommended is to determine and align expectations. He said it is important to understand the expected business results, the company's priorities, and the measures for results. Be sure to clarify the following:

- For what are you responsible?

- What are the immediate expectations and longer-term goals?

- What are your boss's priorities?

- What kind of working relationship does your boss prefer?

- Is anything happening in the organization of which you should be aware?

- Which key people should you meet?

When I was the CEO of a trade organization, I had a new president every year, which meant I had a new boss every year who came with new expectations. I developed a questionnaire I used with each new board president. About a month before the new president took office, I set a time to chat and go over the questionnaire. It gave us both an opportunity to set expectations for the coming year. We clarified our individual roles and goals, and our communication preferences. It was extremely helpful to have a baseline understanding before we launched into the new year.

Once you've gained an understanding of the organizational culture and determined what the company's expectations are, you'll want to turn your focus to early-impact projects, Dolan wrote. You'll want to make an impact as early as possible, he said, so don't dilute your efforts by trying to spend time on every possible project.

Instead, try balancing short-term and long-term focus. Dolan suggested asking yourself three questions:

1. What projects are most important to do in the first hundred days, six months, or year?

2. Which projects are long-term, and which are short-term?

3. Which of the short-term projects are most likely to create an early positive organizational impact?

Depending on your new responsibilities, you may not be in a position to make these determinations on your own. If that is the case, do what your supervisors tell you to do in the order in which they tell you to do it.

The final area Dolan recommended focusing on in the first hundred days is building alliances, relationships, and influence with others. Dolan said you'll want to "establish meaningful and genuine connections with your boss, peers, senior management, customers, and employees to build trust and credibility quickly."

To do this, he recommended understanding the following:

1. For what are others responsible? What is important to them? What do they need? What is their professional background?

2. What works for them? What doesn't? What are their ideas of what should be done to improve things?

3. How does your job fit with what they do? How can you make their job easier?

4. Who are the people in control of the resources that make your work happen?

In the first chapters of this book you learned about personality types, appreciation languages, and strengths. I encourage you to review those chapters and your newly gained knowledge of these topics. Then relate that knowledge to your observations of your new boss and coworkers. Can you get a feel for who on the team are extraverts and introverts? How might you tailor your communication to them? What are your teammates' strengths? Are they giving you any clues as to how they best receive appreciation? Now that you are self-aware, use that knowledge to become more aware of the people you work with and how you can best communicate with and get along with them. I promise, thinking of others will go a long way toward reaching workplace sainthood.

How Am I Doing? Checklist for Success

- ☐ I'm managing negative self-talk by keeping a list of past successes.

- ☐ I have my driver's license and Social Security card in my wallet.

- ☐ I have a bank deposit slip.

- ☐ I have note-taking tools.

- ☐ Thanks to Pinterest, I have a water bottle, snacks, and a sweater.

- ☐ I am prepared to fill out onboarding paperwork because I have the appropriate documents, know how to fill out a W-4, and know the phone number of my emergency contact person.

- ☐ I will keep an open mind about everyone I meet. I will not fall prey to company gossip.

- ☐ I will listen more than I talk, but I won't be afraid to ask questions and clarify instructions.

- ☐ I'm waiting to bring my kitty posters and bobbleheads to work until I know they are acceptable within the organizational culture.

- ☐ I'm learning about my boss and coworkers so I can tailor my communication and get along well with them.

9. What to Do When You Don't Know What to Do

With any new job, you might have downtime during your training. Even though the company is onboarding a new hire, business continues. The person training you may need to deal with a customer, take a phone call, or respond to an urgent message, leaving you sitting alone and wondering what to do.

Whatever you do, resist the urge to take out your phone and get on social media. Absolutely do not take a selfie and post #lookingcutefirstdayatwork!

Instead, consider these productive options:

- Review your notes and jot down any questions, so you're prepared to ask them when training resumes.

- If you are learning how to use company software, practice and note any questions. Ask for clarification when training continues.

- Start reading the employee handbook. Note any questions you might have and ask your boss or HR staff later.

- Read over any available standard operating procedures (SOPs).

- If appropriate, listen in on your trainer's conversation. Learn how they handle customer relations, answer the telephone, or speak with colleagues.

- If you're working retail, familiarize yourself with the inventory.

- If there are posters, signs, or notes on the walls or a nearby bulletin board, read them. Note any questions and ask them when your training resumes.

As long as you're new and learning the ropes, remember to listen more and talk less; focus on understanding, not impressing; and do not refer to what you did on a previous job. In an *Inc.* magazine article titled "13 Ways You Can Immediately Be Productive in Your New Job," consultant Val Wright wrote that job transitions are tough and require "abundant energy, motivation, and perseverance." The author encouraged readers to set realistic expectations, be patient and deliberate, and celebrate their successes along the way.

Progress, Not Perfection

No one expects you to have all the answers on your first day or even your first month on the job. They do, however, expect you to display an interest in your new position and a willingness to learn. Your new boss and coworkers are hoping for progress, not perfection.

My son-in-law is an industrial electrician. He regularly has to show new employees how to perform certain tasks. One guy he works with does not pay attention to his instructions and repeatedly asks for help with the same tasks. My son-in-law has noted that this person is intelligent and able to learn, but he does not seem interested in retaining the information he is given. He doesn't seem to care to do a good job, so Riley no longer cares to help him out.

Initially, Riley was dedicated to helping the new guy become successful. After several months of the man asking for help on the same projects over and over again, Riley has stopped helping. "It's time for him to sink or swim," Riley said. "I have my own job. I can't keep doing his too."

You want your coworkers to respect your work ethic and enjoy working with you. Slacking on the job and refusing to learn how to perform all of your duties is a quick way to become the weakest link and lose support from your team. Bosses notice too.

Kyleen Braxton, owner of Fashion Crossroads Inc. in Casper, Wyoming, said, "Don't always expect to be accommodated. Sometimes you need to take one for the team—sacrifice for your coworkers."

You'll receive some accommodation early in your new position, but after a short while, your boss and teammates will expect you to pull your own weight.

White said she and her team at Adecco are "seeing a lot of people who aren't motivated. They have a huge entitlement mentality." She also said many of today's job seekers do not have life skills or problem-solving skills.

Braxton agreed, saying, "Don't expect to get out of doing certain aspects of the job."

You were hired because you represented yourself in your résumé and interview as someone interested in working for the organization and learning the required tasks.

"No matter what you think," White said, "we don't have to hire you."

But they did hire you. And they trained you. You're receiving regular paychecks for a job you agreed to do. Do it well. And when you don't know what to do, ask.

"Always call me," Braxton reminds staff. "When it's slow and you don't see obvious projects to keep you busy, I always have something you can work on."

White advised taking the opportunities in front of you and staying "focused on what you're doing and don't let anything derail you."

Prove Your Worth

In the last chapter I said these are the top three skills employers seek:

- Critical thinking/problem-solving

- Teamwork/collaboration

- Professionalism/work ethic

Based on White's and Braxton's statements and Riley's experiences with his coworker, it is evident their primary complaints stem from people who lack these top three sought-after skills.

Take a minute right now to list one way you can exercise each of the three skills:

1. To exercise critical thinking and problem-solving in my new job I can ____

    ____

2. I can show teamwork and collaboration by ______________

    ____

3. I can show my professionalism and good work ethic by ________

    ____

Soapbox Alert:

Don't you dare say, "I have no clue."

Nothing gets my blood boiling faster than hearing an employee tell a customer, client, or other stakeholder that they have no clue! This statement makes the speaker sound stupid and causes the recipient to question my ability to train my team. I don't like appearing incompetent. I don't know anyone who does. If you don't know how to do something or how to answer a question, don't say, "I have no clue" or "I don't know." While you are not expected to know everything, you are expected to figure it out.

I learned this lesson the hard way. It was barely a week after my twenty-first birthday and a month into my first "real" job. In other words, it was my first job that didn't involve ironing, babysitting, or flipping burgers. I had landed a job as the periodicals clerk at a community college library and worked the night shift with little supervision. I no longer remember which machine (microfiche or microfilm) had the issue or what needed to be done. Whatever it was, I read the instructions and did not understand them. I tried several times to deal with the issue, and I asked others working that night for help, but they didn't know what to do either. So I put an "out of order" sign on the machine and left a note for my supervisor.

To this day, I regret that I wrote in my note that the instructions were "Greek to me." When I got to work the next day, I found a note from my supervisor. My stomach still knots with anxiety when I think of her scathing response, including the line, "You better learn how to read Greek." Evidently, my "it's Greek to me" statement affected her the same way "I have no clue" affects me.

So, what should you do if you really have no clue? First of all, don't use that phrase. Instead, say something like, "That is an excellent question. Let me look into it and get back to you." Get their contact information, keep your word, and get back to them in a timely manner. Even if you don't find the exact answer, try to at least give them a suggestion of where else they might go. As long as you are polite and professional and show a real interest in resolving the issue, most people will respond in kind and appreciate your efforts.

Keep a record of the questions you receive that you end up having to investigate. It's possible you'll get the same question again. Document your findings, and you'll be ready to confidently answer future requests. This

Q & A log will become a valuable asset for you, your coworkers, and future employees.

By the way, after my experience with the snarky supervisor, I developed a superpower that I have carried into every job since. You see, the reason those instructions were "Greek to me" is because they were written with an assumption of knowledge. Whoever wrote the SOP for those machines already knew how to do what they were writing about and therefore left out some key steps. When I came along, with absolutely no foreknowledge, I couldn't intuitively fill in the missing steps. I ended up rewriting every SOP in the library before I moved on to another job three years later. I have gotten very, very good at writing instructions and SOPs and have written them for every job I've held since that first real adult job. Writing SOPs is a great way to stay busy when you don't know what else to do.

Take Initiative

According to an article in the *Harvard Business Review*, research has confirmed that, when compared to passive employees, "proactive people are better performers, contributors, and innovators." Once you have listened and learned, completed your training, and developed an understanding of the company culture, it is time for you to start showing initiative at work. When you are caught up with your tasks, look around to see what else you can do.

When speaking on the *Andy Stanley Leadership Podcast*, pastor and author Clay Scroggins said, "When I'm only waiting for someone to hand me something, I have the potential to become someone who will not be handed anything."

Scroggins recommended always working to make everything you touch better. "When you focus on making what's in front of you better," he said, "you'll always have something to do."

S. K. Parker and Y. L. Wang agreed that proactivity is highly desired by employers, but they warned that if it's improperly channeled, proactivity can have unintended negative consequences. They analyzed ninety-five employee productivity studies and interviewed twenty-five workers across numerous industries to determine how to be proactive in productive ways. They identified three ingredients for what they call "wise proactivity."

1. **Manage yourself.** The authors encouraged readers to recognize that some problems are not yours to solve. "Taking on too many or too large initiatives can easily lead to burnout," they wrote. They recommended asking yourself the following questions:

    - Which initiatives are worth driving?

    - Do I have enough personal interest and professional expertise to lead one?

    - Do I have the time and resources to execute it?

2. **Consider others.** Before launching into a change initiative, consider how what you are doing will affect others in your workplace. Parker and Wang suggested asking yourself these questions:

    - Who will be affected by my initiative?

    - Whom do I need to onboard to make sure it succeeds?

    - How will I communicate my idea to the most important stakeholders?

- What steps will I take to prepare them?

  The authors said, "Without the support of others, you will likely fail, no matter how proactive you are."

3. **Align your initiative with organizational goals.** If an idea doesn't align with the larger mission of the organization, it will likely be a waste of time and resources, Parker and Wang wrote. The authors suggested asking yourself the following questions before initiating an idea:

- Is the change needed in this situation?

- Is this idea just change for change's sake?

- What type of change is appropriate for this context?

- How can I implement my ideas effectively, given the goals of the organization?

Parker and Wang concluded by encouraging readers to practice wise proactivity. They said it "will help you make the right things happen in the right ways."

If you read the introduction to this book, you'll remember that the first time I caught the boss's attention for proactivity was when I worked at Pep's Drive-In in Torrington, Wyoming. Instead of goofing off between customers, I found ways to keep myself busy that benefited my employer. He noticed and moved me to his café downtown where I was able to work more hours, earn tips, and make more money. It was a winning situation for both Pep and me.

If you want to excel in the workplace, you have to positively set yourself apart from everyone else. One way to do this is to stay busy. When you accepted the job, you entered into a quid pro quo arrangement. You agreed to exchange your time and energies for a paycheck. As long as you're still cashing your checks, your bosses are holding up their end of the bargain. Hold up yours by learning your job, doing it well, and proactively staying busy.

How Am I Doing? Checklist for Success

☐ I am aware of the top three skills employers seek. They are

1. ____

2. ____

3. ____

☐ I have thought about how I can exercise all three skills at work.

☐ I have a positive attitude and a desire to learn.

☐ I have thought about a strategy for handling situations where I don't know the answer. Instead of saying "I have no clue," I will say: _____

____

____

☐ I will keep my word and promptly follow up.

☐ I have started a Q & A file so I can readily retrieve answers to questions to which I did not previously know the answers.

☐ I will practice wise proactivity. These are some ways I can be wisely proactive:

- ____

- ____

- ____

10. The Fastest Ways to Lose Your New Job

This whole chapter is a **Soapbox Alert**! You know that old saying, "Don't get me started!" Well, I'm already started.

The clearest reason people are jerks at work and aren't excelling in the workplace is because they engage in one or all of the behaviors you'll read about in this chapter—or they fail to exhibit the marks of professionalism I mentioned. I think I've been pretty straight so far. So have the professionals with decades of employee management experience.

Just in case we haven't been direct enough for you, I've written this chapter. The topics I'm going to cover in the next several pages are straight answers to what drives employers and supervisors to the breaking point. When we reach that point, you are invited to go home and never come back.

I've already included several pithy quotes from White, but in case you skimmed over them or have forgotten, here's a collection:

- "So many people have no clue how to market themselves."

- "They don't think we are very smart—that we won't find out things about them."

- "We are conducting interviews via Zoom. People aren't dressing for the interview. They look like they just rolled out of bed."

- "No matter what you think, we don't have to hire you."

- "We're seeing a lot of people who aren't motivated. They have a huge entitlement mentality."

Did you see yourself in any of these statements? If you did, it's our hope you recognized what you were doing and made positive changes that led you to this chapter in both your life and the book. You are now employed and hoping to excel in the workplace. You're reading this chapter so you can learn what habits and behaviors to avoid, as well as what professional habits to build.

Overall Attitude

The first topic I want to cover in this chapter is your overall attitude. Employers want staff who have a largely positive attitude. The people you work with and the customers you encounter also prefer to work with positive people. Obviously, we all have bad days. But in general, do you go to work each day with a positive vibe? Do you go to work expecting to have a good day, or do you drag yourself in, determined to be miserable?

Another way to show a positive attitude is to accept responsibility for the whole list of jobs for which you were hired. Your new boss expects you to do the entire job, not just the tasks you enjoy. We all have parts of our jobs we'd rather not do, but if it needs to be done and you're the one hired to do it, get on it! Braxton said, "A job is not a buffet where you get to choose what you will or will not do, when you'll do it, or how you'll do it."

Do the whole job you were hired to do, while exhibiting a cheerful attitude. If you don't, well, we'll find someone who will.

Complaining is a behavior stemming from a bad attitude. Maurie Backman wrote in a 2017 article titled "8 Things You Should Never Do at Work," that "griping to your coworkers on a consistent basis" is a sign you need to change your ways. Backman further stated, "Nobody likes a complainer, but more so than that, the more you moan about the office,

the greater your chances of saying something out loud that could get you into trouble."

Having a positive attitude at work significantly affects your job performance, according to Michele Richinick, who wrote the blog post "Workplace Etiquette: 21 Dos and Don'ts of the Workplace." "Appearing happy, friendly, and approachable at work can do wonders for your career," she said. "Never underestimate the power of a smile!"

Lack of Professionalism

Behaving professionally is still greatly valued by employers, but it is a skill in rapid decline. An article on the website Top Israel Interns, which specializes in career development and advancement and caters to students and graduates seeking internships, asked readers if they are unprofessional without even realizing it. The Top Israel Interns article titled "Hacking an Exceptional Career" stated, "Unprofessional behavior has been marked as one of the leading reasons for employees being fired, and also for potential candidates not being hired in the first place."

The article later referenced survey results from 401 American HR staff on the level of professionalism in new graduates. Here are some of the results:

- 49 percent said fewer than half of new graduates exhibit professional behavior in their first year in the workplace.

- 53 percent said new graduates have a "sense of entitlement," and this attitude is on the rise.

- 43 percent said work ethic among younger employees is worsening, including employees having "too casual" an attitude toward work and "simply not understanding the concept of hard work."

A number of behaviors constitute professionalism. The Top Israel Interns article listed ten. Let's take a look at each one it listed, as well as a few from other sources.

Bad Communication

Written communication, telephone etiquette, and in-person communication hold equal importance. Confusion, arguments, and bad humor can all arise from poor communication. Sometimes you'll encounter bad communication from others, but you can't control them. You can only change your own habits and behaviors.

- **Email**—Respond quickly to emails using a polite, professional tone, and make sure you proofread before hitting Send. Spellcheck is not enough—a computer tool cannot determine appropriate context as well as the human eye. You might have spelled *their* correctly, but did you really mean to use *there* or *they're*? Make sure you spell everything correctly. I stopped doing business with a company because the sales manager allowed a number of typos and grammatical errors in a series of emails we exchanged. The worst was when she continually misspelled the name of the company for which she worked. Regardless of what she meant to tell me in the email, the message I got loud and clear was that she was lazy and incompetent, which meant she would not pay attention to the details of my contract.

  - **Forward**—Be very, very, very careful when replying to or forwarding emails. It can be quite embarrassing to send an email to the wrong person. Depending on the content of the message, you could even lose your job over it. Fortunately, my faux pas wasn't that serious. I was new in my role as an executive assistant. My boss and I had just had a conversation about board members from whom we still needed an RSVP. I went back to my desk, checked email, and chuckled to see I had received a message from one of the people we had just mentioned. Thinking I had clicked the Forward button, I typed, "Speaking of the devil..." and hit Send. A few minutes later, my boss took a phone call from said board member, asking what was being said about him and why he had been called the devil. Talk about mortifying! Fortunately, he accepted her explanation, and we all had a good laugh about it later. If you think you're forwarding a message, slow down and pay attention to whether you have put in the address of the intended recipient. If your email system isn't prompting you for an address, you've probably hit the Reply button.

- **Reply All**—This is another one you need to be extremely careful about. Before hitting Reply All, make absolutely sure you know who is included in the "all" list. Sparks flew between members of two organizations when one person sent a Reply All message to an old email thread. In the new email, the sender wrote something negative about someone from the other company. The sender thought the message was going only to members of their organization, but it actually went to the intended audience PLUS members from the other organization! Yikes!

- **Voicemail/Phone Calls**—Listen regularly to your voicemails and return calls quickly. When speaking to anyone on the phone, maintain a professional demeanor and give your full attention to the caller. Too much multitasking while engaging in business on the phone is distracting. You might find yourself agreeing to something you hadn't intended to, missing an important detail, or leaving the person to whom you're speaking feeling disrespected.

- **General Communication**—Whether it's in writing, on the phone, or in person, professional communication includes the ability to share orders, information, and ideas clearly and effectively. High school teacher Carter Braxton stressed the importance of being able to communicate with a variety of audiences genuinely and effectively. In his profession, it's important that he be able to appropriately customize communications with students, parents, colleagues, and administrators. "Know your audience and be able to adjust your communication to fit," Braxton said. He also advised, "Watch your language—no dropping F-bombs or lewd jokes."

Not Keeping Promises

Be realistic about the deadlines you set for yourself. Create a project list with target dates. Include the target dates in your calendar so you don't overcommit. When you promise to call someone back, send them information, or perform any other task, write it down so you don't forget. People will forgive the occasional need to reschedule or move a deadline, but they'll lose confidence in you if you repeatedly fail to follow through with your promises.

Having Thin Skin

Learn to take negative feedback. None of us likes to hear constructive criticism, but it is necessary for both personal and professional growth. When you receive criticism about your work, whether or not it's justified, control your emotions. Save emotional meltdowns for private moments. And don't go griping to coworkers about the encounter—especially if it was your boss who critiqued your performance. According to the Top Israel Interns article, office politics are "often the result of people being over-sensitive and getting their feelings hurt."

Having thin skin also applies to managing your emotions and which issues in your personal life you bring into the workspace. Kyleen Braxton said, "Don't overshare. I'm your boss, not your friend. I don't need to hear all of that stuff."

That may sound insensitive, but seriously, people! Boundaries have become incredibly blurred in our society. I once had a coworker tell me about her daughter's first experience with feminine hygiene products. TMI, people!! TMI! Just way TOO MUCH INFORMATION! I would not have needed to hear this in a close personal friendship let alone at work from someone with whom I worked part-time!

I'll never forget the final question asked of me during a panel interview thirty-two years ago. The final question was, "We've given you a lot of details about what we would expect of you if you were the successful candidate. If you come to work here, what would you expect of us, your coworkers?"

Wow! What a powerful question! As I progressed in my career and became the interviewer instead of the interviewee, I made a habit of closing every interview with that question. It can be quite revealing. One applicant said that she expected her coworkers to listen to her problems. I'm sorry, but employers don't hire applicants for on-the-job peer therapy. They hire you to do a job. If you need someone to listen to your problems, talk to friends, family, or a counselor you meet with on your own time.

Richinick advised in "Workplace Etiquette" to leave your emotions at home. She wrote, "It's best to leave your personal emotions at the door when you get to work." Spilling your sob story is distracting to your coworkers and reduces your productivity. Richinick recommended taking a personal day if you are so upset you cannot adequately perform your duties.

Stealing

I would assume your mama taught you not to steal but, according to the Top Israel Interns article, thefts of lunches and office supplies are among the biggest complaints HR personnel receive. According to survey results reported by James Weber, Lance B. Kurke, and David W. Pentico in *Business & Society*, ninety-five percent of all businesses experience employee theft, costing companies nearly $52 billion a year.

Stealing comes in a variety of forms, ranging from taking home a ream of printer paper to selling trade secrets or embezzling. One of the most common forms of stealing in the workplace is taking time. Authors of the *Business & Society* article reported that researchers found that on average, workers steal fifty-three minutes a day. Unless you're reimbursing your boss for the time you waste while on the clock, you are guilty of time theft. When you were hired, you entered into an agreement to trade time and energy for a paycheck. During work hours, you owe your boss the time and productivity to which you agreed. They are paying you what they agreed, so you need to hold up your end of the bargain. If you don't, you're a thief.

Here are some ways people steal time at work:

- Repeatedly being late for work

- Leaving early for breaks

- Coming back late from lunch

- Leaving work early

- Conducting personal business while on the clock

- Excessive personal calls and texts

- Too much time chatting about personal issues

- Extra-long potty breaks

- Frequent smoke breaks

- Cyberloafing, which covers all electronic time wasting, including, but not limited to, sending and receiving personal emails, hanging out on social media platforms, online shopping, gaming, and reading non-work-related blogs. According to an article published in *Computers in Human Behavior,* cyberloafing costs organizations up to $85 billion a year in lost productivity. The authors reported employees "spend up to two hours each day engaging in cyberloafing behaviors at work."

We all know you're not a robot. You can't stay on task every second of the day. That's why you get breaks. Maximize them. We also know that a friendly work environment increases productivity. It's OK to chat with coworkers and toss around an occasional joke or personal story. Just be conscious of how much time you're spending off task. Work is your priority as long as you're on the boss's dime.

Not Giving Your Best

Top Israel Interns said nothing stalls your professional growth more than failing to give your best. The unnamed authors stated, "It doesn't help you, and it sure doesn't help the person paying you." They recommended looking for another job if the one you have isn't challenging you or holding your interest.

Sometimes not giving your best occurs because you're unsure of what you're supposed to do. In that case, Richinick recommends asking questions to help clarify expectations and to avoid completing a project or task only to discover you did it wrong.

Gossip

In my experience, gossip is the biggest time waster and the most toxic behavior in the workplace (outside of stealing, lying, and verbal or physical assault). It also runs rampant in the workplace! It is easy to get sucked into office gossip. As stated in the Top Israel Interns article, gossip is a "temporary escape that makes you feel like you're bonding with your coworkers." It isn't healthy bonding. It is an insidious, invasive weed that takes root and is nearly impossible to eradicate once it starts growing. The authors of the Top Israel Interns article minced no words, writing, "It is never OK. It's very unprofessional, it will get you into trouble, and it's just not nice."

I covered this topic in a blog post on my Dandelion Leadership Coaching website titled "Gossips, Liars, and Thieves: What's a Leader to Do?" In that post I shared the following story:

> "I left a job primarily for financial reasons; however, a happy benefit of leaving the organization was getting away from the rampant gossip and negativity. My new boss told me on the first day that gossip would not be tolerated and was grounds for dismissal. When I told a previous coworker this statement, she responded that she wished management at my old job would institute the same policy. I always keep in the back of my mind that if someone is willing to talk about others to me, they are willing to talk about me to others. Gossip, even if the information is true, is detrimental to an organization because it erodes trust and leaves us suspicious of what people are saying about us."

Richinick described gossip as the "cardinal sin of office work." She also said gossiping can "portray you as someone who can't be trusted or someone who isn't a team player."

Gossip can put you in the HR hot seat, according to Backman. Spreading rumors or badmouthing coworkers, supervisors, or your bosses is bad for you in every area of life, but especially in the workplace. Backman said if you really need to "blow off steam, find a friend with an open ear and have those conversations outside the office."

Whatever you do, don't put your gossip in writing! I heard from a trusted friend about someone she USED to work with who had Messenger conversations with another coworker. In one thread, he complained and gossiped about other people with whom they both worked. During a contentious divorce, his vengeful ex-wife printed out the entire digital exchange and gave it to the guy's boss.

Dress

I won't spend a lot of time on this topic because I've already dedicated an entire chapter to the subject (go back and read Chapter 4, if you haven't already). I've included it here, though, because it is one of the areas addressed in the Top Israel Interns article. In the story, the authors recognize that today's workplace has become more casual, but they remind readers that how you dress still matters.

Dressing inappropriately is number three on Backman's list of eight things you should never do at work. "No matter how laid-back your office environment might seem," Backman wrote, "don't make the mistake of wearing clothing that's too revealing, ripped, or just plain unlaundered."

Richinick contended that no one will take you seriously at work if you show up in crop tops, flip-flops, or see-through shirts. She said it's important to dress for success and keep your company culture in mind when you decide what to wear to work each day.

Being Punctual

We talked about being late in the stealing section. The researchers over at Top Israel Interns also listed being punctual as one of the easiest behaviors to exhibit to up your level of professionalism. They wrote, "Being on time shows you respect the people you're meeting with, and also that you value their time as much as your own."

Being punctual encompasses more than just showing up on time for your shift. It also includes being on time for meetings, calling people back when you say you will, and turning in assignments on time. Deadline punctuality goes a long way toward showing your boss and colleagues that you are a professional.

The Blame Game

No one is perfect. It is inevitable that you will make mistakes at work, especially at the beginning of any new job. The more experience you have, both in life and on the job, the fewer mistakes you'll make. But rest assured, you cannot get through life without ever making a mistake.

A sure sign of maturity and professionalism is taking responsibility for your mistakes. Don't try to shift the blame to anyone else, even if the blame can be shared. Own up to your part in the mistake and apologize if necessary.

Once you've owned up to your mistakes, learn from them. Richinick said, "As long as you're constantly growing and learning from those mistakes and make an effort to stop making the same mistake in the future, your coworkers will notice."

Bulldozing

This final sign of unprofessionalism listed in the Top Israel Interns article is a fairly obvious one: "No one likes a bully." However, based on research and reports from employees and employers alike, there is a great deal of dysfunction in the world, including in the workplace.

Workplace bullying is also called workplace emotional abuse or workplace harassment. It is defined in an article in *The International Journal of Human Resource Management* as "subtle and/or obvious negative behaviors embodying aggression, hostility, intimidation and harm." Authors Premilla D'Cruz, Ernesto Noronha, and David Beale said person-related bullying includes "insulting remarks, excessive teasing, spreading gossip or rumors, persistent criticism, intimidation and threats."

Don't be a jerk. It is a myth that the only way to climb the ladder is to squash everyone around you. The article from Top Israel Interns affirmed, "It's much better to work with people who like and respect you than with people who cringe at the sight of you."

Chapter 12 is dedicated to the toxic workplace. In that chapter, I'll quote materials developed by Dr. Paul White, but this seems like a great place to share one of his most jarring yet true statements.

---

*"Achieving great accomplishments doesn't matter much
if everyone who helps you get there dies along the way."*
— *Dr. Paul White*

Lying

We already know that bold-faced lies are unethical and unprofessional. In many cases, out-and-out lies are grounds for dismissal.

But what about white lies? Many people think white lies are appropriate forms of communication in polite society. As I wrote in "Gossips, Liars, and Thieves," "The two primary reasons people tell white lies are because they are uncomfortable with conflict, or they have not been coached and mentored in effectively developing truth-telling skills."

One of the most common times people tell white lies is when they are afraid the truth will hurt someone's feelings. Being honest doesn't mean you have to say everything you think. Sometimes you just need to keep your mouth shut. When you're tempted to tell a white lie, ask yourself if you need to say anything at all.

Another time people tend to fudge the truth is when they fear being found out or getting in trouble. If telling the truth will land you in the hot seat, refer to the section on the blame game. Don't do stupid stuff. Don't shift the blame. Don't lie.

Arguing with Your Boss

I've only fired one person in my career and that's because they argued with me—rudely—in front of other employees. Richinick advises showing respect to your boss by never talking back to them. This doesn't mean you can never disagree. Just maintain a professional, respectful attitude. This is important in all workplace interactions, but especially with the boss. Whenever possible, discuss disagreements with the boss in private.

An article on the Military OneSource website, a resource for service members and their spouses, including education and career opportunities, stated, "Truly collaborative teams work together to find solutions." No two people will agree 100 percent of the time. The secret is knowing how to disagree while staying respectful.

The Military OneSource blog post, "How to Respectfully Disagree with Your Boss " suggested the following:

- Be selective about the issues you decide to bring up with your manager or boss.

- Pick an appropriate time and place to discuss the issues. Schedule a face-to-face meeting. Don't publicly criticize your manager.

- Bring a solution to the table. Supervisors are more likely to validate your concerns if you present a strong argument and a workable solution.

- Start on a positive note. Discuss what is working well before moving on to your recommendations for improvement. Opening the conversation with a negative comment could put your boss on the defensive.

- Know when to let it go. Move on once your supervisor makes a decision. Rehashing issues because you don't agree adds tension to your relationship. Once a decision has been made, suck it up, and move on.

Falling Asleep at Work

This is another category that should go without saying, yet I have four examples of times people were fired because they fell asleep on the job.

This may be the height of unprofessionalism and the absolute quickest way to get fired.

The first time I ran into this scenario was at that library where I supervised student workers. Someone I was working with went to shelve current newspapers and magazines. He was gone for a crazy length of time. When I went looking for him, I found him sound asleep on the floor in front of the newspapers. I didn't have firing privileges, but I certainly reported it to my supervisor.

The next three incidences happened to people I know. A teacher friend told me about a substitute teacher who fell asleep at the teacher's desk. That person was never asked back to the school. Kyleen Braxton found an employee asleep on the couch at the back of her retail store. My final example blew my mind! One of my coaching clients told me about a massage therapist at her workplace who fell asleep while performing a massage! The client complained that when the therapist fell asleep mid-shoulder-kneading, she bonked her head on the back of his head!

Take it from these four unemployed sleepyheads. Falling asleep at work is a bad career move! Practice healthy sleep hygeine by going to bed early enough to get a minimum of seven hours of sleep. See your doctor if you have persistent insomnia or feel tired after adequate sleep. You could have a medical condition that needs treated. I've never fallen asleep at work, but I did go through a period when I was tired no matter what I did. After taking part in a sleep study, I found out I have severe sleep apnea. I feel much better rested and clearer headed now that I received treatment.

Violating Company Policy

Remember when I said to read the employee handbook? This is why: This important governing document clearly states what your employer expects from you. It also makes clear what policy infractions will get you fired. At the time I'm writing this, I have a client for whom I'm conducting an employee handbook evaluation.

This company clearly states in the handbook that the following will not be tolerated:

- Violations of HIPAA laws (HIPAA is an acronym for Health Insurance Portability and Accountability Act, a federal law that protects the privacy of people who seek health care.)

- Theft

- Falsification of company records

- Failure to follow safety practices

- Threatening to do or initiating bodily harm

- Willful or negligent destruction of company property

- Use and/or possession of nonprescription intoxicants, including drugs or narcotics

- Appearing at work after consuming alcohol

These behaviors are often included in employee handbooks. Even if they aren't documented in your company's handbook, don't engage in them. They aren't nice, professional, or in most cases, even legal!

Might Not Get You Fired, But Avoid Anyway

Some things aren't illegal and most likely won't get you fired, but they will tick off your boss and probably get you sent home.

Here's a quick list of dumb stuff to avoid:

- **Coming to work when you're contagious:** We appreciate your dedication to your job, but don't come to work when you're sick and make the rest of us ill, too. Misery does not love company when it comes to viruses. Stay home if you're running a fever, coughing up a lung, or can't get very far from the toilet. Stay away from other people for twenty-four hours after running a fever, vomiting or experiencing diarrhea.

- **Bringing pets to work without permission:** Unless your company has a policy that allows pets on the work site, leave your furry friends at home or at a pet-sitting facility. Even if you have to take Fido to the vet on your lunch break, resist the urge to take him to the office or leave him shut up in your car in the parking lot. Some people are afraid of animals. Others are allergic. And God forbid your pet pees or poops inside! Your pet is a distraction to you and others. Don't bring it to work.

- **Bringing your kids to work without permission:** If your kids is too sick to go to school or day care, they're too sick to bring to work. Take a personal day or drop them off at Grandma's house. Some people take a break to pick up their kids at school and then bring them back to work with them until quitting time. I've had staff members who did this. Their kids sat quietly in their office and got started on their homework. I was fine with this as long as the kids behaved and as long as the employee had cleared it with me first. Some work sites are just too dangerous for kids. Don't bring your kid to work with you if there are any Occupational Safety and Health Administration (OSHA) or other legal prohibitions. These rules are there to keep everyone safe in potentially dangerous environments. Don't risk your job by bringing your kid to work, but more importantly, don't risk your kid's safety!

- **Making appointments during work hours:** Sometimes it's unavoidable. You find yourself having to make a doctor's appointment during the workday. But more often than not, barbers, hairdressers, nail techs, tattoo artists, and other professionals have appointment times before or after work and on weekends. Do your best to schedule personal appointments during nonworking hours. I'm not a morning person, but I always schedule my dental appointments at seven a.m. so I can go before work. If you really can't avoid making appointments during regular work hours, consider scheduling all of your appointments on one day and taking a personal day off work. Just don't try to do this every week—or even every month.

- **Being a slob:** Leaving a stack of dirty dishes or heating up stinky leftovers in the break room is a quick way to annoy your boss and coworkers. Letting the trash can next to your desk overflow. Crumbs in your keyboard. Coffee rings and half-empty soda cans on your desk. Fast-food trash on the floor of the company truck. Cupboard doors and desk drawers hanging open. Failing to empty the shredder when you were the last to use it. Slopping water all over the bathroom sink and mirror. Clipping your fingernails at your desk or channeling your inner Ally Sheedy from *The*

Breakfast Club by raining your dandruff down on the table. Knock it off! Clean up after yourself. Have some self-respect and show consideration for the people who have to work with you.

- **Talking politics or religion:** Unless you work in politics or for a faith-based organization, talking about politics and religion in the workplace can lead to heated discussions. These deeply personal issues strike an emotional chord with many people. Unless you know everyone pretty much agrees with your views, it's best to avoid the subjects altogether. Also, don't assume that just because you work in a traditionally conservative or liberal industry that everyone agrees with your opinions.

You'd be surprised at the shenanigans that go on at work. While drama on TV is entertaining, it's just plain exhausting at work. We've covered a lot of issues in this chapter, but you can avoid getting fired, missing out on a promotion, or receiving an unfavorable review by remembering a few basic lessons you learned in preschool:

1. Be nice.

2. Keep your hands to yourself.

3. Share.

4. Say "Please," "Thank you," and "I'm sorry."

5. Put your toys away, even if you have to sing the "Clean Up Song" under your breath.

6. Don't hit or yell.

7. No name calling or bullying.

8.   Be helpful.

9.   Wash your hands.

Basically, just be a decent human being! You might be surprised how much being nice and doing the next right thing can help you thrive in the workplace. Pay attention to everything in this chapter and clean up your act accordingly, and you'll be able to erase a whole bunch more checkmarks from the Jerk @ Work Checklist. I'm so proud of you for moving from jerk at work or just plain obnoxious. At this point in the book, you should be scoring at mildly annoying or saint. Keep reading to learn how to reach the peak of workplace sainthood.

How Am I Doing? Checklist for Success

☐ I have checked my bad attitude at the door.

☐ I am willing to perform every aspect of what I was hired to do.

☐ I know which behaviors are professional and which are not.

☐ An unprofessional behavior I struggle with is _______________

____

____

☐ Instead of engaging in this unprofessional behavior, I can _________

____

____

☐ If I find myself disagreeing with my boss, instead of arguing, I will __

____

____

☐ The most surprising thing I learned from reading this chapter was

____

____

☐ My most important takeaway from this chapter is

____

____

11. Becoming Indispensable

Have you ever heard of L & D? It stands for learning and development, and it is a big part of your HR manager's responsibilities. In an article on the Toolbox website, the author defines learning and development as "the process of empowering employees with specific skills to drive better business performance." There are other benefits as well, such as employee satisfaction, enhanced employee experience, and increased retention.

Experts typically recommend HR departments follow the 70:20:10 model when they design their L & D strategy, according to the article. This framework suggests that most (70 percent) of an employee's learning happens on the job. They pick up 20 percent of their skills from peers and colleagues, and the final 10 percent through formal training sessions. You are responsible for 90 percent of what it takes to make you indispensable in the workplace. It's up to your employer to provide you with the tools and additional training you need to do the job properly, but it's your responsibility to learn as much as you can and exhibit the qualities of an employee any boss would hate to lose.

Develop Your Followership

One way to take control of your career is to become a great follower. We hear a lot about leadership and what it takes to be a good leader, but we don't hear nearly as much about followership. Every great leader must first be an outstanding follower. In their article, "Followership Development in Adults," Andrew Rahaman and J. Basil Read wrote, "In American society the term *follower* is often met with resistance as parents, teachers, coaches and others in society instruct the young to lead, not follow." They proposed that scholarly descriptions of followers as "those who lack the traits of leaders and passively accede to leader direction" has led to a cultural indoctrination that followership is undesirable.

Rather than considering followership a weakness or something to avoid, the authors assert, "Followership does not mean mere compliance to leader direction, rather it is engaging with the leader to achieve mission-related goals." The first step you can take to become an outstanding follower is to realize you are not a subservient order-taker. You are in a reciprocal relationship with the leadership of the organization and are a proactive contributor to organizational outcomes.

Identify Your Blind Spots

Are you as ethical as you think you are? Most of us consider ourselves to be good people. This implies that, as good people, we are ethical people. In their book, *Blind Spots*, Max Bazerman and Ann Tenbrunsel alert readers to their ethical blind spots. They indicate that we all have a gap between who we want to be and the people we actually are. The authors explained, "The human tendency to make inaccurate predictions about our own behavior is well documented by behavioral ethics and other research."

We are all prone to "behavioral forecasting errors." This means we strongly believe we will act a certain way in a certain situation, but when we find ourselves in that situation, we behave differently.

There are ways you can narrow the gap between your preferred self and your actual self. Bazerman and Tenbrunsel call this "aligning the gap between your 'want' and 'should' selves." The "want" self is the part of us that behaves according to our self-interests, often without regard for moral principles. The "should" self is the part of us that behaves according to values and principles.

The authors offered the following suggestions for removing your blind spots:

- Plan appropriately and reflect realistically on your behavior.

- Project yourself into a future situation; rehearse or practice for an upcoming event.

- Precommit to your intended ethical choice.

- Think about the values and principles that you believe should guide the decision.

- Run your decision through the "mom test"; would you feel comfortable sharing the decision with your mom (or someone else you deeply respect)?

People often say, "You don't know what you'll do until you're in that situation." Well, yes. And no. I think of it like muscle memory. Soldiers, firefighters, police officers, paramedics—they are all examples of people in professions who continually train. They spend many, many hours training so they will "automatically" do what they should in the midst of crisis and chaos. We don't know exactly how we will react in certain situations, but if we plan, train, and practice, we can increase the chances of muscle memory kicking in and taking over for us.

Lead Yourself

I mentioned earlier that we would talk more about self-leadership. In the article, "What Is Self-Leadership? Models, Theory, and Examples,"

Dr. Maike Neuhaus explained the term self-leadership as "the practice of understanding who you are, identifying your desired experiences, and intentionally guiding yourself toward them. It spans the determination of what we do, why we do it, and how we do it." Definitions of self-leadership include elements of self-control, social cognitive theory, and self-determination.

There are eight core competencies and skills for self-leadership:

1. **Self-awareness and self-knowledge**—This is the ability to perceive yourself clearly through inward inspection. Neuhaus said basic self-knowledge is critical for understanding your needs, motives, and drives. It's strongly suggested you explore these four elements:

    - Personality traits

    - Personal strengths and weaknesses

    - Values

    - Talents and interests

2. **Identifying desired experiences**—This involves understanding how to align our goals or desired experiences with our values.

3. **Constructive thought and decision-making**—The human mind is wired to perceive threats, so it is important to practice positivity to help us make rational decisions. "When we are relaxed and in a positive emotional state, we can think creatively and innovatively," Neuhaus wrote. This also includes developing a growth mindset, the belief in our ability to develop and change things or ourselves.

4. **Planning and goal setting**—This involves breaking bigger dreams into manageable milestones, then optimizing each milestone into a goal.

5. **Optimizing motivation**—This includes adjusting one's goals so they become more appealing to us, understanding the role of willpower, and developing self-efficacy by continuously taking small steps toward the goal.

6. **Harnessing the ecosystem**—You can draw support from others in the social, organizational, community, political, and physical environment in which you live.

7. **Amplifying performance**:

   - High-performance planning—Ask yourself questions about how you can perform optimally during a predefined period.

   - Self-coaching—This involves solution-seeking by mentally navigating a coaching framework, such as the GROW model. GROW is an acronym for goal, current reality, options (or obstacles), and will (or way forward).

   - Functional visualization techniques—This includes detailed mental rehearsal of the desired goal behavior.

8. **Embracing failure and cultivating grit**:

   - Practice self-compassion, which means treating yourself with the same care, love, and respect you would give to a close friend who was struggling.

   - Cultivate grit, which is a combination of passion and perseverance for long-term goals. According to Neuhaus,

"Grit is what can, more reliably than any other characteristic, distinguish the successful from the nonsuccessful."

As I have stated before, you are engaging in self-leadership by reading this book. If you went through the first section, you may have already developed the first competency of self-leadership by learning about your personality type, strengths and weaknesses, and appreciation language.

On the *Andy Stanley Leadership Podcast,* Pastor, author, podcaster, and leadership expert Clay Scroggins offered four tips for becoming indispensable in the workplace. His tips correspond well with the eight competencies previously discussed. Scroggins had these suggestions:

1. **Lead yourself**—learn to be a great follower. Those who lead themselves are the quickest ones to get promoted.

2. **Choose positivity**—but not to the point of being naive or blind to serious issues. Remember that even a look, eye roll, or shrug can derail decisions and reduce positivity.

3. **Think critically**—This requires a mental shift from thinking like an employee to thinking like an owner. Scroggins gave an example of two people who are walking down the hall and see a wadded piece of paper on the floor. The person in employee mode walks past the trash with the mindset "It's not my job" or "That's not my problem." The owner, or an employee thinking in owner mode, sees the paper and stops to pick it up and put it in a trash bin. Those who have owner mentality take pride in their workplace and do whatever is necessary to take care of the organization. Scroggins also said thinking critically involves being present in the moment while thinking.

4. **Resist passivity**—Don't wait for others to get it together. Work on what you can.

There are many things you can do to strive toward the goal of making yourself indispensable at work. Just keep in mind that no one is ever truly irreplaceable. Learn everything you can in your job, maintain a positive attitude, be a great follower while effectively self-leading, and watch out for those blind spots, and you'll at least make your boss and coworkers exceptionally sad to see you go if that time ever comes.

How Am I Doing? Checklist for Success

☐ My role as a follower is ___________________________

____

☐ I admit that I may have ethical blind spots.

☐ An area where I would like to narrow the gap between my "want" self and "should" self is ___________________________

____

☐ The steps I will take to narrow the gap are

- ___________________________

- ___________________________

- ___________________________

☐ I will work on developing the following competency for self-leadership ___________________________

____

☐ One way I can develop this competency is ___________________________

____

☐ I can choose positivity by ___________________________

____

☐ One way I can think more critically is ___________________________

____

☐ One way I can resist passivity is ___________________________

____

SECTION 4:
FINISHING WELL

Back in the *Leave it to Beaver* days of Ward Cleaver, dads worked at the same company for thirty years and moms stayed home and managed the family. According to a Bureau of Labor Statistics (BLS) report issued on October 7, 2020, the average American held 12.3 different jobs before they turned fifty-three. The BLS report indicated that nearly half of those were before age twenty-five, compared to 2.9 jobs from ages thirty-five to forty-four and 1.9 jobs between the ages of forty-five and fifty-two. I guess it takes a while to figure out what we want to do with ourselves.

Ward probably mowed lawns and delivered newspapers as a kid, then, after college, he went to work for the company from which he would retire thirty years later. It's likely Ward wrote one résumé, went to a few interviews, and then never thought about job searching again. Those of us in today's workplace probably won't have that luxury. We will change jobs many times before we retire—if we choose to do so.

Another difference from the 1950s is we now live in a global community. We have a saying in my home state, "Wyoming is one small town with really long streets." With fewer than six hundred thousand people in the entire state, we're likely to run into people we know anywhere we go. Certainly, we will meet someone who knows someone we know. That's one of the reasons I make a habit of being careful what I say about anybody, especially employers and coworkers. You never know when you'll end up working with some past coworker's cousin or a former boss's spouse. Easily accessible travel, internet communications, and social media platforms have opened the world up like one small town with really long streets. Just today I had a "Wow! It's a small world!" moment when my niece changed her relationship status on Facebook. She's from Baltimore, Maryland, and attends college in Wyoming. Her new boyfriend is from New Jersey and attends the same Wyoming school. I've never met him, but it turns out he and I have a mutual friend on Facebook. His cousin is a friend who lives in New York whom I met during our first doctoral program residency!

Never overlook the importance of keeping up professional relationships with former employers and colleagues. When you decide to change jobs, do it with class and don't burn bridges. You may need a reference, want to come back to work for the company, or end up marrying your former office mate's fourth cousin once removed. In this final section we'll take a look at reasons you may decide it's time to move on, how to search for another job while still employed, and how to leave your job in good standing. Here's to finishing well!

12. Toxic Workplaces

So far in this book we have covered the importance of knowing yourself in order to better market yourself. In the next section we talked about the nuts and bolts of job hunting, primarily résumés, cover letters, and interviews. Then we explored ways to set yourself up for success in your new job and how to grow into a valued employee. In this final section of the book, we will explore how to know when it's time to leave and how to do that well.

The two most-cited reasons for quitting are pay and conflicts at work. While you don't need to read a whole chapter about the pros and cons of changing jobs for a higher paycheck, a chapter on taking care of yourself in an unhealthy environment might prove helpful.

We begin every week with 168 hours. For those employed full-time, a minimum of forty of those hours are spent in the workplace. If you sleep eight hours and work eight hours, you have eight hours left each day to shower, commute, prep and eat meals, and all the other things you need to do every day. One-third of most days is spent at work with coworkers. Healthy work environments foster greater productivity and produce less stress. It's great when you like the people you work with and enjoy going to work. But seven of ten US workers say they are either going through the motions or straight up hate their jobs.

According to Gary Chapman, Paul White, and Harold Myra, the authors of *Rising Above a Toxic Workplace*, toxic and healthy workplaces often have similar mission statements. Both express values that include integrity, respect for individuals, and commitment to excellence. The difference lies in what behaviors each type of organization allows. The authors stated, "Positive organizations find ways to put their stated values into action, but toxic cultures allow personal agendas and other priorities to crowd out what they declare in print."

Founders have the privilege of setting the desired tone of their business. When they start their company and hire their first employees, they set the tone for how everyone behaves in the workplace by the way they treat their staff. It's like that saying, "You reap what you sow." In every relationship, including those with bosses, managers, and coworkers, the work environment is only as healthy as its sickest member.

Healthy Workplace Environments

"Healthy workplaces," according to Chapman, "grow from high mutual respect and sensitivity to others." We all need to feel appreciated and be treated with respect. Employees and managers who express appreciation and kindly confront concerns before they have a chance to fester help build a healthy work environment.

In healthy workplaces, people take fewer sick days and are less likely to quit. People talk, joke around, smile, and help one another out. Team Building Made Easy posted an article on their website titled, "9 Signs Your Company Has a Healthy Workplace Culture." Those nine signs are:

1. Communication is strong.

2. People speak positively of one another.

3. Feedback is provided regularly.

4. Staff retention is high.

5. Leadership encourages mobility (i.e., promotions).

6. Staff spend time together outside the office.

7. Everyone feels they have a purpose.

8. People want to be a part of your team.

9. Humor is encouraged and commonplace

Every work environment has times of stress. How those stressful times are handled says a great deal about the health of the environment.

Toxic Workplace Environments

Toxic workplaces have a higher turnover rate and more absences. If you've always been pretty healthy, but now you're getting a lot of colds and flus, it could be that your immune system has weakened due to the chronic stress of working in a toxic environment. Gossip; criticism; and coworkers who constantly complain, lie, and fail to do their share of the work are all behaviors that lead to a toxic workplace. Take a look at this checklist from *Rising Above a Toxic Workplace:*

1. Hidden agendas characterize communication and decision-making; issues aren't openly addressed.

2. Departments seldom work together to reach shared goals.

3. Leaders have the pattern of saying one thing and doing another.

4. Everyone feels pressured to make things look good.

5. The managers view people as there solely to get tasks done, with little interest in getting to know them personally.

6. Supervisors or managers manipulate team members through embarrassment or anger.

7. Apathy, cynicism, and a lack of hope mark the overall work environment.

8. Rules and procedures are largely ignored.

9. Employees sense little accountability for their own actions and decisions.

10. People are used for the organization's benefit and discarded when no longer considered useful.

Did you recognize your workplace in any of these ten signs of a toxic workplace?

Top Traits of Toxic Leaders

It may be your boss or your boss's boss, but it's possible the toxicity at work is coming from a toxic leader. Here's a list of top traits toxic leaders exhibit. This list is adapted from *Rising Above a Toxic Workplace.*

- **They look good (at least initially):** I had a toxic boss who I'd been told looked great to the board who hired her. After they fired her and hired me to replace her, one of the people who had been in her interviews said she had a great résumé and interviewed very well. The authors of *Rising Above a Toxic Workplace* said toxic leaders are often "articulate, skilled socially, and persuasive. They may be physically attractive, have an impressive résumé, or come from a famous or successful family." The authors further stated that in some cases, these individuals start out largely healthy, but over time, "pressures and compromises degrade their integrity."

- **They are extreme about achieving goals:** They get stuff done, but their goals are driven by self-interest and self-promotion. They will use the organization's resources to help them achieve their personal objectives.

- **They're manipulative:** They manipulate both information and people. They are especially good at making things look good when they're not. They manipulate through the use of guilt, shame, and threat of embarrassment.

- **They're narcissistic:** They truly believe they are better than everyone around them. They believe rules don't apply to them because they have a higher purpose. They also imagine they are the reason for everything good that happens in the workplace and therefore they should get the credit.

- **They steal the credit for others' successes**: They will take full responsibility for any success or something that looks successful.

- **They're condescending:** They expect to be served by others, regardless of the person's position. When they don't feel appropriately respected, they tear down those they see as a threat.

- **They're inauthentic:** At first, they may act as if they care deeply about the organization's cause and its people, but over time, their true persona becomes apparent.

- **They use others:** For the sake of "the larger cause," they will use and sacrifice those who work for them, no matter how loyal they are. They rarely take responsibility for anything that goes wrong.

- **They won't address real risks:** They tend to ignore issues they don't care about or those that don't help them look good.

- **Before things fall apart, they leave:** Most toxic leaders are good at leaving before things fall apart. They move on to another job, often into a higher position of leadership, and leave everyone else to deal with the ruin they left behind. The person I mentioned earlier had started covering her behind by putting the blame for her failures into my personnel file. If I hadn't gone back and taken her job after she was fired, I never would have known she had lied about me and my performance.

If you think you're working for a toxic boss, the authors suggest finding ways to nurture your inner reserves, gain perspective, and develop toughness. Stay positive, resist retaliations, and don't let bad leadership turn you bitter. Don't take your frustrations with your boss out on those you work with or your family. Do what you can to keep the poison from reaching others.

Before you decide to quit your job because of your boss's bad behavior, consider these tips from Lachlan Brown, author of *Toxic Bosses: How to Deal With Them Before They Ruin Your Life*:

- **Protect yourself mentally**: Internalize the message that you are not at fault. The most dangerous thing bullies and abusers do is convince you that you are alone. Seek out others on your side and tell yourselves that this is not your fault.

- **Protect yourself legally**: Keep records of everything. If your boss promises you a few days off, a raise, a short break, or anything else, get it on the record.

- **Relax in your time off**: Learn to relax as soon as you get off work. I used to think that venting to a friend about the bad stuff at work was a healthy way of dealing with it. Actually, the more I talked about it, the more worked up I got, and the less I enjoyed my free time. Don't keep it all bottled up, but don't dwell on it. Focus on your friends, family, hobbies, or anything else that brings you joy.

- **Accept their behavior:** Don't get caught in the idea that it will change. The sooner you accept it, the sooner you can plan strategies to move forward.

- **...But don't blame them**: Toxic people want their behavior to be justified. Brown cautioned against lashing out at them. This just gives them what they want. Brown advised, "Don't give them the satisfaction, and learn not to blame them for their behavior... Learn to ride it out until you can leave or move above them."

- **Learn to work with them:** without triggering their immature behavior.

If your boss's toxic behavior continues and is making your life miserable, you'll have to make a decision. Do you want to keep putting up with it, report them to HR, or move on?

It's Not Me, It's You

This entire book has been dedicated to equipping you with the knowledge you need to improve your performance in the workplace. Chapter 10 was dedicated to behaviors likely to get you fired. At this point, you have enough tools to assess your own behaviors and decide if you are the toxic employee (the jerk at work). If you're stressed out at work and thinking about quitting and you have already determined you're not contributing to the toxicity, it may be time to leave. Before you turn in your notice, consider these suggestions from *Rising Above a Toxic Workplace*:

- **See through the fog:** Seek clarity about what's really going on.

- **Ask yourself the tough questions**: Are you giving up too soon? Have you studied the principles for dealing with bad bosses and awful jobs? Unlimited resources are available online.

- **Assess your options**: Do a careful assessment of all your possibilities. Network for insights and options.

- **Listen to your body.** If your mental and physical health is compromised, it might be time to change jobs.

- **Face joblessness head-on**: "Whether you're in a workplace that's empowering or exploitive, summon courage and a readiness to view whatever happens as the next set of challenges and the next adventure."

If your Sundays are spent dreading Monday, you might be in a toxic workplace. You shouldn't have to spend one-third of your life in misery. You'll learn more in the next chapter about how to decide when it's time to leave your job and how to do it professionally.

How Am I Doing? Checklist for Success

☐ This chapter was interesting, but everything is great at work. (Yay! I'm so happy for you!)

☐ I think I might be a toxic employee. My toxic behaviors are

- ____________________________

- ____________________________

- ____________________________

☐ Now that I realize I'm contributing to the problem, I can do the following to improve:

- ____________________________

- ____________________________

- ____________________________

☐ I have a toxic boss. Before deciding to quit, I'll try the following:

- ____________________________

- ____________________________

- ____________________________

☐ I have a great boss, but the culture at work is still toxic. Some
possible reasons:

- ____

- ____

- ____

☐ To help improve the health of my work environment, I will

- ____

- ____

- ____

13. Should You Stay or Should You Go?

Have you outgrown your position with no chance of promotion? Are you ready for a new challenge? Did you recognize your situation in the toxic workplaces chapter? Eventually, as they say, all good things must come to an end. It may be time for you to apply the KonMari method to your employment.

Marie Kondo is a professional organizer and minimalist who literally wrote the book on decluttering. She is known for teaching people to tidy by category, not location, and ask one soul-stirring question: "Does this item spark joy in my life?" If it doesn't, get rid of it.

It's a great concept, to a point. Ideally, we would all focus on what brings us joy. Realistically, there are some things we just have to have and some things we just have to do, whether or not they spark joy. Doing dishes and cleaning toilets do not spark joy for me, but they are not tasks I can simply declutter from my to-do list. They are essential. It's the same with a job. Not every aspect of your job is going to spark joy. I do think, though, that it is a good exercise to examine all elements of your job and decide what sparks joy and what doesn't. Then you can make a more informed decision about whether it's time to stay or to go.

When I was trying to decide whether I would leave my last job, I pulled out a tablet and pencil and started journaling. I made several lists:

- What I still hoped to accomplish at my current job

  - After making this list, I estimated how long it would take me to accomplish each goal. This exercise led to an estimate of how much longer I needed to stay at the job. Would I

> accomplish all I set out to do in only a year or did I have enough goals to keep me going to retirement?

- If I never do these things again, it will be too soon (stuff I hated)

  - After I wrote this list, I looked at each item and considered whether I could eliminate, delegate, or outsource the task.

- What I loved about my current job

- Things I loved from each job I'd ever had

- Things I hated from each job I'd ever had

After completing all of these lists, I looked for the common denominators. I sought patterns as I reviewed my entire work life. What areas had I enjoyed across the board? What tasks had I hated doing at every job? Once I identified the patterns, I was able to determine my key areas of interest, as well as what I considered drudgery.

This exercise helped me realize that while I loved much about my job, some nonnegotiable elements of it were keeping me in perpetual stress. I also realized that I had checked off all of my priority projects from the list I'd made when I was hired and that my passions had since shifted. I was ready for new challenges in a different sector.

If you think it might be time to move on, but you aren't quite sure, give this exercise a try. Maybe you'll be reenergized by your list of things you still want to accomplish. Perhaps you'll find tasks you dislike that you can delegate or outsource. If you like your job and the people with whom you work, but feel like you need more challenges, consider talking to your boss. Ask if there are opportunities for growth. If you are a good employee, most employers would rather work with you than lose you.

Before making the decision to leave a job, Mandy Day-Calder recommends weighing the pros and cons. She counsels employees to take a step back from their emotions and think about "what you want to do, what you are qualified to do, and what you can afford to do." She also recommended writing down all of the pros and cons of your current job on a weekly basis for a month or two. This will help you avoid having your "perceptions tainted by particularly draining shifts."

Quitting a job is not a decision best made in the heat of the moment. Emotions can be fleeting and deceiving. In an article on the Wall St. Watchdog website, author Sam Becker recommended considering these four thoughts before deciding to quit.

1. **Don't do it on a whim:** "There are very few situations in which having no job is better than having a job you dislike," Becker wrote. Theoretically you're hoping for a better, more fulfilling position. If you quit in a fit of anger or extreme fatigue, you may be forced to take any old job just to pay the bills.

2. **Are you chronically unhappy or unfulfilled?:** There's an old saying, "Wherever you go, there you are." Is a change of job going to resolve your unhappiness, or is something within you keeping you from feeling happy or fulfilled? If you have unresolved issues, changing locations may not have a lasting effect. After all, wherever you go, you take yourself and all your problems and insecurities with you. If you're truly unhappy in your current situation, it is important to understand what parts of your current job are making you feel that way. If you can identify the unhappiness factors, you can avoid shifting to another job where you're equally miserable.

3. **Have you given it a good go?:** You owe it to yourself and the people who spent valuable time and money hiring and training you to give your current position a fair shot. Giving up too soon is just as damaging to your career as staying too long in a dead-end job.

4. **Could the situation be resolved without such drastic action?:** Chances are that your coworkers are frustrated by the same issues you struggle to embrace. Before throwing in the towel, have a conversation with your supervisor. Go into the meeting armed with solutions. Don't just gripe about things without offering ideas for improvement. Who knows, maybe your positive attitude and suggestions will make a difference for you and everyone else.

Heather V. MacArthur specializes in writing about "navigating the unspoken rules in today's workplace." In a 2019 Forbes article, "Top Tips for Deciding Whether It's Really Time to Quit Your Job," she shared several great bits of wisdom.

1. **Know your purpose:** When we throw ourselves 150 percent into our jobs and expect work to fill all of the holes in our lives, we set ourselves up for failure—and burnout. I know because I've been there. After my youngest child moved out, I was left with no one to go home to. My friends were all married and busy with their families. I started spending my evenings at the office and finally heading home around eight p.m. with a pile of work. I'd sit on the couch in front of the television and keep on working—only with my feet up. Even when I took vacation days, I never truly shut it off. During one of my annual reviews, the board president told me they appreciated my dedication to the organization but that I received more vacation days than my staff because I was in a higher-stress position. He said, "A healthy you is of more value to us than a tired and sick you." I should have lis-

tened. A few years later, I came to a full realization of what he had hoped I would avoid. Years of blurred boundaries and workaholism left me physically and emotionally burned out. One way to avoid this scenario is to know your greater purpose. MacArthur suggested getting clear on what you want out of life and then allowing work to support that instead of the other way around. Look for hobbies or volunteer opportunities that spark joy in your soul. I've heard leaders in the faith community say, "Consider what breaks your heart that also breaks the heart of God. That's your purpose." My friend Gayle loves animals and is passionate about pet rescue and adoption. She's also a writer. She has combined these two loves to create a successful freelance writing and speaking career. Her job supports her passions. She has a purpose outside of punching a time clock.

2. **Check for burnout**: MacArthur indicated that many factors can lead to burnout. As examples, she mentioned lack of variety, neglected self-care, or unfulfilling workloads. Take your vacation days, get outside and breathe fresh air, start a fitness regimen, and don't work through lunch. Yoga is one of my favorite stress relievers. I can rush into class, exhausted and distracted, but balance takes concentration. It's impossible for me to hold tree pose if I lose focus. As soon as my mind starts drifting to my troubles, my balance drifts too. If I don't catch myself and refocus, I'll fall completely out of the pose. Another thing that helped me through burnout was learning about my personality type (see Chapter 1) and how personality and stress are related. Once I understood how I was wired and what my natural tendencies were, I was able to forgive myself for not being as tough as I thought I should have been. Then I was able to learn to recognize my stress triggers and how to move back into balance. If you would like

to know more about stress and type, contact me about TypeCoach or check out *Was That Really Me?* by Naomi L. Quenk.

3. **Identify what would make you want to stay:** MacArthur said to think about what would make you *want* to stay vs. just being *willing* to stay. She suggested thinking about more than just a pay raise. Consider how you would like to feel every day when you walk into work. Fantasize about your ideal role in the organization and the related job responsibilities. How would you like to relate to those on your team? After dreaming about the ideal scenario for you to stay where you are, brainstorm how you can take steps to make that wish a reality.

4. **Create more of what you want where you are:** No one cares as much about you and your career as you do. You can't sit around waiting for those in the chain of command above you to make your career dreams come true. As we discussed earlier in this chapter, if you're considering leaving a job, think about what changes would make you happy about staying. Then schedule a meeting with your supervisor and chat about the options for growth available to you.

5. **Don't quit because you don't get along with someone:** Leaving for this reason is a stellar example of self-sabotage. Quitting doesn't heal the rift between you and your coworker; it just leaves you without a job! If you're otherwise happy at your job, don't let the annoying behaviors of a coworker run you off. Instead, look at what it is about the coworker that's driving you to the breaking point. Just like when we talked about identifying stress triggers so you can learn to refocus, it is beneficial to recognize what triggers you to dislike another person. MacArthur rightly said, "The probability of running into people who trip you up in the same ways at your next workplace is pretty high. After all, it's not the person, but the way they behave that is

triggering you." Learn to work through your irritations and develop your interpersonal skills.

The decision to leave a job you worked so hard to land is not an easy one. Reasons to leave are as varied as the types of jobs and people who hold them. When my kids were little, my husband and I had a pretty sweet schedule going. We were able to always have one parent at home with the kids. Then his shift changed to a schedule that would have had us working during the same hours. I looked into day care, and the cost for two kids would have cost more than I made at my job as a staff writer at the local newspaper. My husband made significantly more money than I did, so it made sense that I would be the one to quit my job. When I told my boss, he tried to work with me, offering to give me more hours. While I loved the work, it didn't make financial sense to hand my entire paycheck over to a day care. We did work out a small solution in that I did some freelance work for the newspaper. It kept me writing, but I was able to work around time with my kids.

I left one job because my family moved to another state. I left another because I was able to move into a position at another company that doubled my income. By that time, I was a single parent, so more money and health benefits were a game changer. I left another job because of a toxic boss. A few months later, they fired her and called me to take her place—ah, karma . . .

I'm sure you can see my point. There are many, many reasons to leave a job. Life happens; circumstances change. Research published in *Labour Economics* indicated dissatisfaction with pay and/or job security are the most important factors leading to employee decisions to quit. Other significant reasons for quitting included dissatisfaction with the work itself, work hours, and the use of initiative. Whatever your reasons for resigning, consider all of your options before writing your resignation letter or storming out in a cloud of anger. I've always told my kids the cheapest car to drive is the one you already own. (I think finance talk show host Dave Ramsey might have said that before I did.) There are a lot of extra expenses when you trade cars—stuff like taxes, new license plates, and increased insurance rates for a newer car. It's the same with changing jobs. There are always hidden costs, both economic and emotional. Changing jobs might include uprooting your life and moving to another town, state, or even a different country. Even if you stay in the same place, you might have to increase commute times, get a new wardrobe, or brush up on skills through additional training. It also takes time and energy to search for a new job, including sending out résumés and going to interviews. Before you leave your current job, weigh the costs and consider whether you're ready to invest the time, energy, and money it takes to transition to a new position.

If you decide it is time to move on, keep reading for helpful tips on finishing well. How you leave a job is just as important as how you find one.

How Am I Doing? Checklist for Success

Unless you checked this book out from the library or borrowed it from your boss, this is a safe space to journal your way through the process of deciding whether you should stay or go. Consider the following questions and write your answers here, on a separate piece of paper, or on your digital device.

- Am I just having a bad day, week, or month? If I hang on a while longer, will circumstances improve?

- Do I want to quit because of a personality conflict with my boss or a coworker?

- What triggers a negative reaction to the person with whom I'm struggling to get along?

- How can I learn to change how I react to these triggers?

- Am I nearing or in full-on burnout?

- What behaviors can I change to put out the burnout flames? Do I need to start taking my lunch break, using vacation days, and leaving work on time? Do I need to practice more self-care?

- If I could do anything in the world, what would it be?

- What do I love about my current job?

- What do I hate about my current job?

- What tasks on my hate list can I eliminate, delegate, or outsource?

- What would it take for me to want to stay at my current job?

- What do I need to do to change my attitude or my circumstances to make going to work trigger a spark of joy?

- What goals do I still want to accomplish at my current job? Does looking at this list inspire me to stay?

- Have I learned everything I can in my current position? Do I have nowhere else to go within the organization?

- If I leave my current job, what would I rather do? Would I stay in the same city, state, or country?

- What would it take to equip me for my next dream job? What training? What experience?

- Have I tried talking to my boss about what is making me unhappy in my current position? How did that conversation go? Was there a resolution or confirmation that I need to move on?

- I have decided it's time to go. Now what? (Psst, keep reading).

14. Exit Right

You have given it serious consideration. You took time to use the journaling prompts at the end of Chapter 13, and you've come to the conclusion that it is time to move on to a different job. The next thing you have to decide is how you want to end things. Every article I read, journal I searched, employer I interviewed, and friend I chatted with said the same thing about leaving a job: Give notice and exit gracefully. As far as I'm concerned, giving notice is one way of exiting gracefully. While it may be tempting to channel your inner David Allan Coe and tell your boss to "take this job and shove it," how you choose to leave may impact your long-term career. This is the last chapter of the book, and the last chapter of your story at your current place of employment. Write a happy ending and exit right by considering the following tips.

Quit First or Find a New Job First?

Can you afford to leave before you have another job lined up, or do you need to find a new job before you can leave? If you're thinking about quitting before you have something else secured, consider the following questions:

- How much money do you have in savings?

- How long can you afford to remain unemployed?

- How much are you willing to tighten your budget so you can afford to be unemployed?

- Do you want to take some time between jobs to travel or go back to school?

- Are you burned out? Do you need time to restore yourself?

Quitting First

In his *Wall Street Journal* article, "How to Quit a Job and Leave on Good Terms," Anthony DeRosa stressed the importance of having your finances in order before quitting, especially if you plan to take some time between jobs. He shared the following tips for considering the financial ramifications of quitting your job:

1. Find out when you'll receive your last paycheck and if you will be eligible for unemployment benefits.

2. Check to see how long your health-care coverage will remain in effect and whether you can obtain health insurance through alternative avenues such as COBRA. COBRA is an acronym for Consolidated Omnibus Budget Reconciliation Act. Basically, COBRA is a federal mandate that allows you to purchase the health insurance provided through your employer for up to eighteen months after you leave the company. Check the costs before you decide to quit your job and go with COBRA. Under COBRA you pay the entire premium, including the share your employer now pays.

3. Decide what to do with your 401(k), if you have one. Will you pay a tax penalty and cash it out or roll it over into an Individual Retirement Account (IRA)?

4. Consider any other benefits you receive from the company, such as life insurance. Are the benefits portable (meaning you can take them with you if you take over payments), or will you lose them when you leave? My last job provided a cell phone for me. When I left, I bought out the contract and transferred the phone to a personal account. Think about all of your current perks and how you will replace them when you leave.

Jim Wang's advice in "8 Questions You Must Ask Before Quitting Your Job" overlaps with DeRosa's tips. Additionally, Wang encourages readers to have an emergency fund, even if they plan to move directly into another job. There is always the possibility the new job won't work out and you'll end up unemployed. There also may be a lag between your last paycheck at one job and your first payday at the new job. Financial advisers traditionally advise stockpiling three to six months of living expenses in your emergency fund. Wang concurs, considering three months to be the absolute minimum to have saved before you resign from your current position. If you're moving into self-employment, dropping from a dual to a single income, or quitting before you find another job, Wang recommends having closer to a year's worth of living expenses accumulated.

Finding a New Job First

Job hunting while still clocking in at the job you've decided to leave is a delicate situation. DeRosa cautioned job seekers to be discreet and conduct their searches as quietly as possible. Save the phone calls, emails, and résumé writing for your personal phone and computer. DeRosa also reminded readers to "avoid using your employer's phone, email, or computer to job-hunt."

My HR friend Kaitlin offered the same advice. She said, "Don't job search on the company computer. Don't save your résumé on the company computer. Don't check email or voicemail during work hours."

When you start scheduling interviews, try to set them up for your lunch hour or before or after your shift ends. Most hiring managers will understand and do their best to accommodate you. They will appreciate your conscientiousness and commitment to your current employer. Asking to schedule an interview during times that don't interfere with your current responsibilities should send a positive message to potential employers that you are seeking a new position the right way.

If you have a good relationship with your current supervisor, Kaitlin said it's OK to have a conversation about your decision to move on. Perhaps you have an opportunity to pursue a lifelong dream, or you want to move. Kaitlin recommended being up-front and letting them know a change is coming. "It's OK to share," Kaitlin said. "They're only going to be an advocate for you."

Only you truly understand the climate of your current situation. You'll have to use your discretion in deciding whether to let your current supervisor know you're planning to move on. Research published in 2016 and reported in the Newstex Finance and Accounting blog identified seven distinct ways people quit their jobs.

Researchers Anthony Klotz and Mark Bolino published their findings in the *Journal of Applied Psychology*. They listed the following ways employees resign. The first four patterns are positive and acceptable. Unless you're really looking forward to getting the "you'll never work in this town again" promise, avoid the last three ways of quitting.

1. **By the book:** According to Klotz and Bolino, about 31 percent of employees choose to go with this standard method of resignation. It typically involves giving two weeks' notice. This form of resignation is the most preferred by employers and often includes a face-to-face conversation and written letter of resignation. The employee is open about their reason for leaving.

2. **Perfunctory:** The second most common way to quit is exercised by about 29 percent of those leaving a position. They follow the basic framework of "by the book" but do it carefully, with almost surgi-

cal precision. They do not elaborate on why they are leaving or share their future plans. Becker called this the "it's not you, it's me" way of quitting.

3. **Grateful goodbyes**: About nine percent of job quitters really like the people they work with and want to make the process as painless as possible. Becker stated the grateful goodbyes method is "a positive and grateful way of bowing out and helping your old team deal with the loss."

4. **In the loop**: This is the method Kaitlin meant when she said you can tell your supervisors if you already have a good relationship with them. Researchers described this approach as a situation where "a boss or employer is aware that an employee will soon be leaving." In these cases, the employee might intend to change career tracks or go back to school. About eight percent of those who quit use this method.

5. **Avoidant**: Becker compared this method to breaking up with your significant other over text message. Sending in your notice or resignation through the human resources department, a third party, or over the weekend and then avoiding seeing your boss or old team again is the epitome of an awkward breakup. It's often difficult to quit a job, but avoiding the other party is a cowardly way to end any type of relationship. Don't do it. It's not cool. I've heard a number of examples from HR friends and fellow bosses of people who texted messages like "I quit" or "I found a new job; I won't be in." According to the research, about nine percent use the avoidant method.

6. **Impulsive quitting**: In four percent of cases, people reach their breaking point, blow up, and walk out. I call this the "Take This Job

and Shove It" method. You can guarantee you won't get a good reference from your boss if this is how you end things.

7. **Burning bridges**: Seven-time New York Times best-selling author and nationally syndicated newspaper columnist Harvey Mackay is credited with saying, "Unless you work in demolition, don't burn bridges." The burning bridges method of quitting (ten percent) is similar to the impulsive quitting but not as explosive. According to Becker, "This is when you might tell your boss to chug bleach or to play in traffic. You're not planning on maintaining any type of rela-

tionship after you leave, so you might as well make a few enemies on the way out."

Leaving gracefully

We've talked about what you need to consider before deciding to quit and covered the seven most common methods. I've encouraged you to be discreet while job searching before you resign and encouraged you to make a graceful exit. But what if you really hate your job and can't wait to move on? All the more reason to practice grace and discretion. Thomas Heath, author of *The Washington Post* article, "How to Quit a Job You Hate with Grace," offered a few rules to abide by on your way out the door. These tips apply to leaving under any circumstance because whether you hate your job or love it and are sad to leave, you should do your best to leave on good terms. You may want to use colleagues as references. Perhaps you live in a small town or work in a small industry. Your reputation precedes you. Protect your reputation by taking the high road and leaving on good terms.

1. **Stay off social media**: According to Heath, "Too many people give into their negative feelings on the way to their next job and commit career suicide by trashing their former employer." As an employer, if I look at your social media feeds and see you have posted complaints about your other jobs, coworkers, and/or boss, I will swipe left on your application.

2. **Give notice**: Depending on what your organization requires, the best practice is to tell your boss in person and follow up with a written letter of resignation. Give as much notice as possible. MacArthur said people often ask her if they have to give two weeks' notice. She likes to respond, "No, you could give more." The higher you are in

leadership, the more notice you should give. When in doubt, refer to the company employee handbook. Most handbooks outline the process for resigning. It is common for employers to include a statement requiring written notice. In some cases, there is a policy that if you want to be eligible for rehire, you must give written notice. You may think you hate your job and will never want to work there again, but you never know what might happen. Remember that toxic boss I mentioned? With her gone, I was happy to go back. Fortunately, I had given notice both in person and in writing and had left on good terms with colleagues and board members. Had I left in a huff, burning bridges behind me, I never would have gone back as the CEO and grown significantly, both personally and professionally.

3.   **Craft a clear story**: Heath suggested working with your employer to decide when and how your colleagues will be notified that you're leaving. ALWAYS tell your boss about your decision to leave FIRST. Don't tell your best work buddy or anyone else. News travels fast.

4.   **Say thank you**: Heath said just because you are leaving the company doesn't mean you're leaving all of your relationships. Thank mentors, sponsors, and others with whom you've built healthy relationships. Make a plan to stay in touch.

5.   **Have a transition plan**: Don't leave your team or employer in a pickle. Kaitlin said you should work to leave your position in good hands. She recommended making sure your SOPs (standard operating procedures) are up to date and your file system organized—and remember you are leaving behind your reputation. "People form opinions of you based on how you leave the way for others," Kaitlin said.

6. **Work until your last day**: Once an employee has decided to leave a job, it is common to mentally and emotionally check out. You're still getting paid to do a job, so earn your pay. Heath said to "focus on delivering quality work until your last day." Stephanie Stephens, author of "Prove You're Not a 'Quitter': First and Last Job Impressions Count," said, "Don't slack off on your deliverables." In fact, Stephens added, "The truly valuable employee will actually kick things into high gear during the last period of work," so they don't leave a mess for those they leave behind.

There are a lot of things to remember as you transition from one job to the next. Don't forget this list of don'ts compiled from several of the afore-mentioned resources:

- Don't just stop going to work without formally quitting.

- Don't text your resignation.

- Don't go on vacation and then just fail to come back.

- Don't speak negatively about your experience.

- Don't leave without offering notice—period.

- Don't slack off on your deliverables.

- Don't feel obligated to give details about your next move.

- Don't send dramatic farewell correspondence.

- Don't spoil the relationships you've built over time.

- Don't tell your boss or coworkers what you really think of them (even if you think they deserve it).

- Don't damage company property.

- Don't take any physical or intellectual property belonging to the employer.

- Don't blame others for your unhappiness.

Now, let's end on a positive note by considering this list of dos:

- Do try to resign in person.

- Do give notice. Two weeks is standard, but as Kaitlin said, "Even a week is fine. It's better than not giving any notice."

- Do gather your personal items (remember your coffee cup and leftovers in the fridge; no one should have to throw out your spoiled food items after you're gone).

- Do clear your browser history and remove autocompletion for logins and passwords on company computers.

- Do continue to collaborate and partner with others.

- Do provide contact details.

- Do clean up your space and personal information.

- Do return all company-owned property such as tools, uniforms, or keys.

- Do be professional and honest and finish your assignments on time.

- Do ask for a reference that may help you in the future.

- Do keep your options open.

- Do consider all sides of a story that involves you.

- Do leave the past behind and embrace the future.

- Do tell your colleagues how much you appreciate them.

- Do thank your boss, supervisor, and/or mentor.

- Do leave good feelings in your wake.

Making the decision to leave your job is difficult. It's sometimes exponentially harder to work up the courage to tell your supervisor or boss that you've decided to move on. I don't think I will ever get comfortable with telling someone I have decided to quit. Knowing how to do it well is half the battle. We may not enjoy saying goodbye, but at least we can live with integrity and leave gracefully.

How Am I Doing? Checklist for Success

☐ I have a transition plan.

☐ I have decided to

    ○ Quit before I have another job lined up

    ○ Find a job before I turn in my notice

☐ I have examined my financial situation and made the following decisions:

    ○ I have an emergency fund to cover living expenses for

        ⌗ three months

        ⌗ six months

        ⌗ one year

        ⌗ Other: ___________________________________

    ○ For health care I will

        ⌗ Purchase COBRA

        ⌗ Have coverage at my new job

        ⌗ Other: ___________________________________

- ○ For retirement I will
    - ⌑ Roll my 401(k) into an IRA
    - ⌑ Take the tax penalty and cash out
    - ⌑ I don't have a retirement account through my current job
- ○ I will receive my last paycheck on ____________________________

☐ I will use the following resignation method:

- ○ By the book
- ○ Perfunctory
- ○ Grateful goodbyes
- ○ In the loop

☐ I will give notice in person and follow up with written notice.

☐ I will give the following notice:

- ○ One week
- ○ Two weeks
- ○ Other: ____

☐ My last day will be ____

☐ Before I leave, I must complete the following projects:

-    ____

-    ____

-    ____

-    ____

-    ____

-    ____

CONCLUSION

Whew! We've covered A LOT of material on our journey from jerk to saint.

I recently had a chance to chat with two of my friend's daughters. We were laughing about some memories when the youngest reminded us of when she and her sister snuck out of the house.

"I was more scared of you than I was my mom!" she said.

I was shocked by this statement. My son tells everyone that I am as soft as a down comforter. He says I'm not the scary mama bear I'd like people to think I am, that I'm really just a big old teddy bear.

When I asked her why she was more afraid of me, she said, "Because you say exactly what you think."

She's right. That is something I do. You might have noticed that as you read this book.

"Well, that's because I love you." I said. "If I think you're acting like a jerk, I'm going to tell you you're acting like a jerk."

Even though I don't know you, I wrote this book because I care about you. I want you to do well. I want you to know that there isn't enough time to make all of the mistakes in this world, so you can learn from mine. And if you've been acting like a jerk, I'm telling you to knock it off! Stop acting like a jerk.

Now that you've read this whole book and worked through the exercises, I encourage you to go through the Jerk @ Work Checklist at the beginning of the book one more time. Go ahead. I'll wait . . .

How did you do? Did you make it to saint? It's OK if you scored mildly annoying or even downright obnoxious the second time. At least you're not a jerk. It's a process, and it takes time to change old habits. Keep working at the topics in this book and before long you'll realize you've learned how to quit being a jerk at work.

I'm so proud of you!

REFERENCES

Andel, S. A., Kessler, S. R., Pindek, S., Kleinman, G., & Spector, P. E. (2019). Is cyberloafing more complex than we originally thought? Cyberloafing as a coping response to workplace aggression exposure. *Computers in Human Behavior*, 101(2019), pp. 124-130.

Arndt, A. D., Evans, K. R., Zahedi, Z. & Khan, E. (2019). Competent or threatening? When looking like a "salesperson" is disadvantageous. *Journal of Retailing and Consumer Services.* 47(2019), pp. 166-176.

BasuMallick, C. (2020, June 12). What is learning and development (L&D)? Definition, objectives, and best practices for strategy. *Toolbox/ HR.* https://www.toolbox.com/hr/learning-development/articles/what-is-learning-and-development-objectives-strategy/.

Becker, S. (2016, August 26). Wall street cheat sheet: How to quit a job: The 7 ways employees hit the bricks. *Wall St. Watchdog.* Chatham: Newstex. https://www.wallstwatchdog.com/money-caree/ways-employees-quit-jobs/.

Beebe, J. (2012). Psychological types in Freud and Jung. *Jung Journal, 6*(3), pp. 58-71. https://doi.org/10.1525/jung.2012.6.3.58.

Brown, L. (2019, December 26). Toxic bosses: How to deal with them before they ruin your life. https://hackspirit.com/toxic-bosses/.

Buckland, M. (2014, August 14). 25 fun facts about résumés, interviews and social recruitment. Business 2 Community. https://www.business2community.com/human-resources/25-fun-facts-résumés-interviews-social-recruitment-0975676.

Buxman, K. (2020). *Lead with levity: Strategic humor for leaders*. Levity Works Publishing.

Chapman, G. & White, P. (2012). *5 languages of appreciation in the workplace.: empowering organizations by encouraging people*. Revised and undated. Chicago: Northfield Publishing.

Chapman, G., White, P., & Myra, H. (2014). *Rising above a toxic workplace: taking care of yourself in an unhealthy environment*. Chicago: Northfield Publishing.

Clendon, J. (2020, November). Talking about unconscious bias. *Kaitiaki Nursing New Zealand, 26*(10), pp. 32-33.

Day-Calder, M. (2017). Weighing up the pros and cons before you quit your job. *Nursing Standard (2014+), 31*(36), p. 35.

D'Cruz, P., Noronha, E., & Beale, D. (2014). The workplace bullying-organizational change interface: emerging challenges for human resource management. *International Journal of Human Resource Management, 25*(10), pp. 1434–1459.

DeRosa, A. (2020, Dec 02). How to quit a job and leave on good terms. *Wall Street Journal (Online)*.

Dolan, B. (2019). Transition into a new job. *FEMS Microbiology Letters, 366*(5).

Doyle, A. (2020, January 20). Hard skills vs. soft skills: What's the difference? The Balance Careers. https://www.thebalancecareers.com/hard-skills-vs-soft-skills-2063780.

Doyle, A. (2020, September 17). Interview question: "Tell me about yourself." The Balance Careers. https://www.thebalancecareers.com/tell-me-about-yourself-job-interview-question-2060956.

Doyle, A. (2020, September 17) *What is business casual attire?* https://www.thebalancecareers.com/what-is-business-casual-attire-2061168.

Doyle, A. (2020, October 19). *How to write an interview thank-you letter.* https://www.thebalancecareers.com/how-to-write-an-interview-thank-you-letter-2063981.

Eschleman, K. J., Bowling, N., & Zelazny, L. (2020). Getting a grip on the gripers: Curmudgeon personality's relationships with job attitudes and employee well-being. *Personality and Individual Differences.* 167(2020) 110253, pp. 1-7.

Flanagan, J. L. & Lewis, V. J. (2019). Marked inside and out: an exploration of perceived stigma of the tattooed in the workplace. *Equality, Diversity and Inclusion: An International Journal.* 38(1), pp. 87-106.

Flaum, J. P. (2018). When it comes to business leadership, nice guys finish first. *Green Peak Partners,* p. 5. https://greenpeakpartners.com/wp-content/uploads/2018/09/Green-Peak_Cornell-University-Study_What-predicts-success.pdf.

Flowers, A. (2017, May 26). 12 things to never put on a résumé. *Blue Sage Career Strategies.* https://bluesagecareers.com/blog/2017/5/26/12-things-to-never-put-on-a-résumé ?rq=12%20things%20to%20never%20put%20on%20a%20résumé.

Garrido Vásquez, M. E., Garrido-Vásquez, P., & Otto, K. (2020). Two sides of workplace interactions: How appreciation and social stressors shape the relationship between job insecurity and well-being. *Europe's Journal of Psychology, 16*(3), pp. 458-478.

Greenly, G. (2020, March 25). Gossips, liars, and thieves: What's a leader to do? [blog]. *Dandelion Leadership Coaching.* https://www.dandelionleadershipcoaching.com/post/ learn-how-to-free-yourself-from-anxieties-with-these-8-easy-steps.

Grobelny, J., Frontczak, P., Pawlak, K., Skorodzillo, U., Szymanowska, M. & Wilczynska, S. (2020). A conceptual model of the influence of résumé components on personnel decisions: A policy-capturing study on résumé screening. *Journal of Management Information and Decision Sciences.* 23(2), pp. 57-78.

Gurden, D. (2016). Make an impression. *Nursing Standard (2014+), 30*(21), p. 63.

Gurung, R. A. R., Brickner, M., Leet, M., & Punke, E. (2018). Dressing "in code": Clothing rules, propriety, and perceptions. *The Journal of Social Psychology,* 158(5), pp. 553-557.

Hacking an exceptional career: Are you unprofessional? (N.D.) *Top Israel Interns.* http://topisraelinterns.com/are-you-unprofessional/.

Hamrick, N., & White, P. (2020). Specific acts of appreciation valued by employees. *Strategic HR Review, 19*(4), pp. 163-169.

Heath, T. (2017). How to quit a job you hate with grace. *The Washington Post (Online).* https://www.washingtonpost.com/news/business/ wp/2017/01/04/how-to-quit-a-job-you-hate-with-grace/

Heathfield, S. M. (2020, June 30). *What is business attire?* https://www. thebalancecareers.com/what-is-business-attire-1918075.

Hickman, A., & Evans, M. C. (2018, March 27). How do Clifton-Strengths and the VIA survey compare? https://www.gallup.com/cliftonstrengths/en/249878/compare-via-survey-cliftonstrengths.aspx.

Horton, A. P. (2017, July 26). These are the worst answers to the most common job interview questions. *Fast Company.* https://www.fastcompany.com/40442242/hiring-managers-reveal-the-worst-answers-to-the-most-common-job-interview-questions.

Howlett, N., Pine, K. J., Cahill, N., Orakçioğlu, I., & Fletcher, B. (2015). Unbuttoned: The interaction between provocativeness of female work attire and occupational status. *Sex Roles, 72*(3-4), pp. 105-116.

How to land your next job. (2019). *Canadian Journal of Medical Laboratory Science*, 81(1), p. 10.

How to respectfully disagree with your boss. (N.D.). https://myseco.militaryonesource.mil/portal/content/view/1471.

Hurwitz, M. & Hurwitz, S. (2020). Integrating followership into leadership programs. *New Directions for Student Leadership.* 167(Fall), pp. 23-35.

Interview questions: What are your greatest weaknesses? (2021, January 11). *Indeed.com.* https://www.indeed.com/career-advice/interviewing/interview-question-what-are-your-greatest-weaknesses.

Jones, D. (2005, Aug 05). Study says flirtatious women get fewer raises, promotions: [FINAL edition]. *USA Today.*

Koay, K. Y. (2018). Workplace ostracism and cyberloafing: A moderated–mediation model. *Internet Research,* 28(4), pp. 1122-1141.

Kholin, M., Kueckelhaus, B., & Blickle, G. (2020). Why dark personalities can get ahead: Extending the toxic career model. *Personality and Individual Differences*. 156(2020) 109792, pp. 1-7.

Lee, Sung Ho (2018, June 19). *Your guide to the different types of business attire* https://www.michaelpage.com.au/advice/career-advice/starting-out/your-guide-different-types-business-attire.

MacArthur, H. V. (2019, February 19). Top tips for deciding whether it's really time to quit your job. Forbes.com. https://www.forbes.com/sites/hvmacarthur/2019/02/19/top-tips-for-deciding-whether-its-really-time-to-quit-your-job/?sh=4cb5c2645147.

Mathews, J. (2018). Inside Cubitts: Lead optometrist at Cubitts, Jewlsy Mathews, discusses the importance of the cover letter and how a little research can go a long way. *Optometry Today (London), 58*(6), p. 88.

MBTI Basics. https://www.myersbriggs.org/my-mbti-personality-type/mbti-basics/.

Meagher, K. A. (2017). An examination of the recruitment selection factors for a front desk agent. *Journal of Human Resources in Hospitality & Tourism, 16*(2), pp. 171-191.

Miglianico, M., Dubreuil, P. Miquelon, P., Bakker, A. B., & Martin-Krumm, C. (2020). Strength use in the workplace: A literature review. *Journal of Happiness Studies*, 2020(21), pp. 737-764.

Milosevic, I., Maric, S., & Loncar, D. (2020). Defeating the toxic boss: The nature of toxic leadership and the role of followers. *Journal of Leadership and Organizational Studies*. 27(2), pp. 117-137.

Moran, G. (2018, April 19). *Why You Need to Pay Attention to Gen X Leaders.* The Future of Work [blog]. Fast Company. https://www.fastcompany. com/40558008/why-you-need-to-pay-attention-to-gen-x-leaders.

Neuhaus, M. (2020, November 11). What is self-leadership? Models, theory, and examples. https://positivepsychology.com/self-leadership/.

Niranjan, D. (2005). Starting a new job in SH&E: Tips for a successful integration. *Professional Safety, 50*(6), pp. 36-40.

Number of jobs, labor market experience, and earnings growth: Results from a national longitudinal survey. (2020, October 7). *Bureau of Labor Statistics* [news release]. https://www.bls.gov/news.release/pdf/nlsoy.pdf.

Oberai, H. & Anand, I. M. (2018). Unconscious bias: thinking without thinking. *Human Resource Management International Digest.* 26(6), pp. 14-17.

Parker, S. K. & Wang, Y. L. (2019, August 21). When to take initiative at work and when not to. *Harvard Business Review.* https://hbr. org/2019/08/when-to-take-initiative-at-work-and-when-not-to.

Peluchette, J. V., & Karl, K. (2007). The impact of workplace attire on employee self-perceptions. *Human Resource Development Quarterly, 18*(3), pp. 345-360.

Pfister, I. B., Jacobshagen, N., Kalin, W., & Semmer, N. K. (2020). How does appreciation lead to higher job satisfaction? *Journal of Managerial Psychology.* 35(6), pp. 465-479.

Prohibited Employment Policies/Practices. U.S. Equal Employment Opportunity Commission. https://www.eeoc.gov/ prohibited-employment-policiespractices.

Rahaman, A., & Read, J. B. (2020). Followership development in adults. *New Directions for Student Leadership.* 167(Fall), pp. 27-45.

Rath, T., & Conchie, B. (2009). *Strengths based leadership.* Gallup Press.

Rennung, M., Blum, J., & Göritz, A. S. (2016). To strike a pose: No stereotype backlash for power posing women. *Frontiers in Psychology, 7,* p. 1463.

Richinick, M. (2020, April 17). Workplace Etiquette: 21 Dos and Don'ts of the Workplace. *Northwestern University Graduate Programs* [blog]. https://www.northeastern.edu/graduate/blog/workplace-etiquette/.

Riggio, R. E. (2020). Why followership? *New Directions for Student Leadership.* 167(Fall), pp. 15-22.

Rose, N. (2020). Four CV mistakes and how to correct them: Director of CV writers, Neville Rose, on the mistakes that people make on their CV and what you can do to avoid falling foul of them. *Optometry Today (London),* 60(1), p. 89.

Ruch, W., Proyer, R. T., Harzer, C., Park, N., Peterson, C., & Seligman, M. E. P. (2010). Values in action inventory of strengths (VIA-IS): Adaptation and validation of the German version and the development of a peer-rating form. *Journal of Individual Differences,* 31(3), pp. 138-149.

Smith, J. K., Liss, M., Erchull, M. J., Kelly, C. M., Adragna, K., & Baines, K. (2018). The relationship between sexualized appearance and perceptions of women's competence and electability. *Sex Roles, 79*(11-12), pp. 671-682.

Stanley, A. (2017, July 6). *How to Lead When You're Not in Charge – Part 1*. Andy Stanley Leadership Podcast. https://podcasts.apple.com/us/podcast/andy-stanley-leadership-podcast/id290055666?i=1000309566990.

Stanley, A. (2017, August 3). *How to Lead When You're Not in Charge – Part 2*. Andy Stanley Leadership Podcast. https://podcasts.apple.com/us/podcast/andy-stanley-leadership-podcast/id290055666?i=1000309566990.

Stephens, S. (2014). Prove you're not a 'quitter': First and last job impressions count. *Biomedical Instrumentation & Technology, 48*(6), pp. 441-4.

Sullivan, J. (2013, May 20). Why you can't get a job: Recruiting explained by the numbers. [blog]. DrJohnSullivan.com. https://drjohnsullivan.com/articles/why-you-cant-get-a-job-recruiting-explained-by-the-numbers/.

Team Building Made Easy. (2021, August 20). *Company Workplace Culture: 9 Signs it is healthy* https://www.teambuildingmadeeasy.com.au/9-signs-your-company-has-a-healthy-workplace-culture/

Testman, J. (N.D.). *8 Phone Etiquette Tips for Job Seekers.* https://ssv.org/blog/2019/1/8/8-phone-etiquette-tips-for-job-seekers.

Tews, M. J., Stafford, K., & Kudler, E. P. (2020). *Journal of Personnel Psychology*, 19(1), pp. 4-13.

TheEmployable: How to know when to quit your job (2015, May 12). *Newstex Global Business Blogs*. Chatham: Newstex.

Tomkovick, C., & Swanson, S. (2014). Using Strengthsfinder to identify relationships between marketing graduate strengths and career outcomes. *Marketing Education Review*, *24*(3), pp. 197–212.

Thomas, T. & Berg, P. (2020). The Army paradox: Leader and follower education. *New Directions for Student Leadership*. 167(Fall), pp. 111-122.

Thompson, R. (2020). Followership identity work. *New Directions for Student Leadership*. 167(Fall), pp. 65-75.

Toomey, R. & Toomey, C. (2017). *Type Descriptions*. TypeCoach, LLC.

Toomey, R. & Toomey, C. (2018). *Temperaments and motivation* [presentation notes]. TypeCoach, LLC.

Unknown author. (n.d.) *Finding the Golden Mean*. https://www.viacharacter.org/pdf/GoldenMean.pdf.

Wang, J. (2020, February 26). 8 questions you must ask before quitting your job. Forbes.com. https://www.forbes.com/sites/jim-wang/2020/02/26/8-questions-you-must-ask-before-quitting-your-job/?sh=4a6f9d5b9a5d.

Weber, J., Kurke, L. B., & Pentico, D. W. (2003). Why do employees steal? Assessing differences in ethical and unethical employee behavior using ethical work climates. *Business & Society*, *42*(3), pp. 359-380.

Wiafe, N. (2020, February). Interview skills: Your guide to winning at job interviews. *Nursing Standard*, *35*(2), pp. 40-41.

White, P. (2016). Appreciation at work training and the motivating by appreciation inventory: Development and validity. *Strategic HR Review*, *15*(1), pp. 20-24.

White, P., Hamrick, N., Hepner, T., & Toomey, R. (2019). How personality type and languages of appreciation interrelate. *Strategic HR Review, 18*(1), pp. 2-7.

Wilson, K. (2018). Write a résumé that stands out. *Chemical Engineering Progress, 114*(1), p. 21.

Zambas, J. (2018, June 5). How to answer the most common illegal interview questions. https://www.careeraddict.com/illegal-interview-questions.

Zestcottt, C. A., Tompkins, T. L., Williams, M. K., Livesay, K., & Chan, K. L. (2018). What do you think about ink? An examination of implicit and explicit attitudes toward tattooed individuals. *The Journal of Social Psychology*, 158 (1), pp. 7-22.